SCARED
SPEECHLESS

SCARED
SPEECHLESS

9 WAYS
TO OVERCOME YOUR FEARS
AND CAPTIVATE YOUR AUDIENCE

STEVE ROHR and
DR. SHIRLEY IMPELLIZZERI

CAREER
PRESS

Pompton Plains, N.J.

SCARED SPEECHLESS
EDITED BY ROGER SHEETY
TYPESET BY PERFECTYPE, NASHVILLE, TENN.
Cover design by MTWdesign
Printed in the U.S.A.

To order this title, please call toll-free 1-800-CAREER-1 (NJ and Canada: 201-848-0310) to order using VISA or MasterCard, or for further information on books from Career Press.

The Career Press, Inc.
12 Parish Drive
Wayne, NJ 07470
www.careerpress.com

Library of Congress Cataloging-in-Publication Data

CIP Data Available Upon Request.

We dedicate this book to Steven Villescas, Jr., who is unwavering in the belief that anything is achievable through hard work and an open heart, and proves it every day.

Acknowledgments

This endeavor would never have been possible without the enormous love and support of some wonderful people. Tony Sweet and Ann Walker at Universal Broadcasting Network generously gave us a platform to explore the intersection of psychology and everyday life. One topic we covered is our primal fear of public speaking, which sparked the idea for this book. We'd like to give a special thanks to our radio show production team, who made the real magic happen: John Williams, Natalia Renteria, and Gabe Harder. Marilyn Atlas, our fearless literary manager, believed in the project from the beginning and took it to our agent, Mike Farris, who found the perfect home for it at Career Press.

Steve Rohr is indebted to his high school competitive speech coach Myrna Watson, who helped him realize he had a voice and used it to win two consecutive individual state championships. He will be forever grateful to his college coaches Dr. Cindy Larson-Casselton and Dr. Cynthia Carver for their extraordinary guidance. In remembrance of the late Daryl Koenig, who gave Steve the opportunity to deliver the biggest speech of his life, which opened up the biggest door. Additionally, coaching the Arizona State University speech team as a graduate assistant under the tutelage of Dr. Clark Olson offered Steve his first opportunity to guide students to national championships. Further, he is especially thankful to Dr. Chris Freeman whose fine friendship and world-class advice never falter. Finally, to his mom, Lois Burgdorfer, whose unconditional love and limitless encouragement always makes the impossible, possible.

Dr. Shirley Impellizzeri would like to thank her first two mentors, Dr. Lawanda Katzman-Staenberg and Dr. Paul Abramson, who saw her potential before she could see it in herself. She will be forever grateful to Dr. Peter A. Levine and Dr. Dan Siegel, who taught her everything she knows about the brain-body connection. A special thanks to her little Sydney, who is now five feet taller than her mom, and continues to amaze her with her fearless and compassionate spirit. And to Jackie, who is forever encouraging and a wonderful support.

Contents

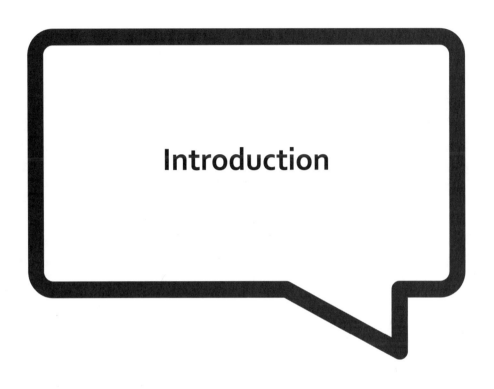

Introduction

Public speaking is the #1 fear in America. Death is second.

Yes, we'd rather *die* than give a speech. We'd also be more willing to get stuck in small spaces, make nice with spiders, or slither with snakes. That's why millions have made it a mission to avoid public speaking at all costs. Perhaps you're one of them! By luck or crafty maneuvering, you managed to evade that "mandatory" public speaking course in school. Professionally, you've also deftly defied the *need* to speechify by conveniently "volunteering" others or hiding in the bathroom. You know who you are! Maybe you've tried to conquer your fears. You took a class, went to a workshop, read books, or watched training videos to shake your nerves. Despite your very best efforts, nothing worked and you're back to square one. We've got big news:

You're not alone and it's not your fault. There are real reasons why nothing has worked.

First, you've been flat-out lied to. Anyone who tells you that nerves can completely disappear doesn't know much about how the brain works. Not only is this scientifically unsound, it automatically assumes nerves are *bad*. In fact, nerves are *great!* We'll show how this can be and how to handle yours when public speaking.

Second, like many people, you've probably been misled by myths. However, some of the most popular ideas about public speaking (for example, imagining your audience in their underwear) are not only borderline creepy, they actually compete with your true nature, which ultimately prevents you from realizing your full potential as a speaker. Consider what this "underwear" advice conveys: "Audiences are scary and to be avoided" and "Whatever you do, don't connect with them in a genuine way." We think both of these claims are showstoppers, and not in the good way. It's because we know for a fact that audiences are *not* your enemy. On the contrary, unless you're in a prickly political debate, all audiences *want* you to succeed. We know it's hard to believe, but after we tell you why, you will never look at the audience as an adversary again. Further, failing to build a real rapport with your audience defeats the entire point of public speaking. Again, you might see this as the perfect hack, but in fact, it just holds you back.

Third, no matter what you've read, it was most likely written by someone whose primary expertise *isn't* public speaking. Bona fide academic public speaking experts write college textbooks almost exclusively. So don't expect to find an advanced degree in speech communication and any formal teaching experience among the authors of general market public speaking books. Don't get us wrong. We're not saying these writers aren't experts in their respective fields; they're just not specialists in public speaking. Many of these fine folks have a strong business background or make a living giving motivational speeches, but success in business doesn't make you an authority on public address. And just because you can deliver a speech, doesn't mean you can teach others to do it. Think of it this way: If you need a wisdom tooth pulled, you'd want someone trained in dental surgery to do it, right? So why settle when it comes to public speaking?

The other reason we believe these resources don't deliver real results is that they miss a critical component of public speaking: how your brain factors into the equation. In essence, we believe the *why* has always been short-changed by the *how* when it comes to public speaking. For instance, we're all in such a hurry to "get over being nervous" that we don't bother asking why we're nervous in the first place, hence, the inspiration to envision our audience in their skivvies. However, understanding the *why* of your behavior is absolutely critical to becoming an authentic, confident, and powerful speaker. *Scared Speechless* explores the intriguing intersection of speech communication and psychology, and shows that by understanding your brain (the why), you can evolve into an authentic, confident, and powerful speaker (the how).

The idea for this book developed from a discussion on our "psychology meets real life" radio show. Given our respective areas of expertise (communication and psychology), we explained why public speaking is so scary and how you can use that knowledge to your advantage. While researching for the show, we found studies explaining the psychology of public speaking and resources on how to give a speech, but nothing that combined these two crucial elements in any significant way. We noted this surprising fact during the episode. After the show aired, several listeners urged us to write a book expanding on this information. We looked at each other and said, why not? After all, we love what we do and have spent our entire academic and professional careers dedicated to the practical application of our fields.

Please allow us a little bragging here: Steve gave his first public speech in first grade to a very distracted kindergarten class. Despite the lukewarm response from his fidgeting audience, he was hooked on talking. In high school, he was a two-time high school state speech champion and received a speech scholarship to attend Concordia College (Moorhead, MN). As a competitor, he won several speech titles and was ranked one of the "top 10" college speakers in the nation. Upon graduation, Steve gave the student commencement message to an audience of 8,000 faculty, parents, and students. He received a standing ovation, the first time ever for a student in the college's 100-year history. A few years later, he gave a 20-minute keynote speech to 38,000 high school students in the Superdome (New Orleans) and received another standing ovation. He earned his master's degree in communication from Arizona State University. As an educator, Steve has been privileged to teach speech communication at four community colleges as well as coach several national speech champions, some of whom had no prior public speaking experience. Due to their success, many received scholarships to some of America's most prestigious universities. He has also taught public relations at Loyola Marymount University and California State University, Long Beach. Additionally, Steve is the show publicist for the Academy Awards and founder of a Los Angeles–based entertainment PR agency.

Dr. Shirley became curious about human behavior after taking a psychology class in high school. She began to wonder what made people so different and, at times, so alike. Given that, she thought studying psychology in college was the perfect way to find out. After receiving her bachelor's degree in psychology from UCLA, she knew this was the career for her and went on to earn her PhD in psychology still as a Bruin. However, her thirst wasn't fully quenched, which led to many postgraduate studies. What came to interest her most was the field of neuroscience, how the brain works. Suddenly, everything came together; human behavior made sense and so did she. In 2012, she shared her story in a best-selling debut book. In it she explains how the brain works, why we behave the way we do, and how to change what isn't working for us. Television audiences know her from frequent appearances on shows like *The Doctors* and *Dr. Drew*, where she advises on a range of psychology topics.

You might be scared speechless at the moment. That's understandable. But now it's time to figure out why. In *Scared Speechless*, we're going to turn what you think you know about public speaking completely upside down and then inside out. Our approach works and we know it can absolutely work for you. So buckle up as we explore public speaking in a wholly fresh way. Oh, and get ready to give the best speech of your life!

Steve Rohr, MA
Shirley Impellizzeri, PhD
Los Angeles, CA

Chapter 1
You've Got Some Nerve

According to most studies, people's number-one fear is public speaking. Number two is death. Death is number two. Does that sound right? This means to the average person, if you go to a funeral, you're better off in the casket than doing the eulogy.

—Jerry Seinfeld

<u>**Chapter Focus**</u>

How to make fear your friend (or at least not your *foe*).

Why you're programmed to panic.

Stage Flight

Public speaking is the great *equalizer*. Just ask Hollywood movie director Michael Bay. Bay's numerous films, including the *Transformers* franchise, have grossed almost $8 billion at the box office worldwide.[1] Yet, even with this formidable experience "calling the shots," the famous director fled the stage at a 2014 Las Vegas electronics show after getting flustered during a presentation for the media. Bay blamed a faulty teleprompter and later wrote on his Website: "I just embarrassed myself."[2] We're not sharing this story to pick on Bay. But his mumbled fumble goes to show that even titans can topple under public speaking pressure. The truth is that effective public speaking is *scary* no matter who you are or where you're from. Sure, parts of public speaking (preparation or performance) might come easier for some, but no one is born with a silver tongue in their mouth. Effective public speaking is a *learned* skill. And when you reach your potential as a speaker, life can be a lot more interesting and rewarding.

Career experts will tell you that strong public speaking skills give you an edge in the workforce. Even if you work in a field like IT or engineering, at some point, you will be asked to give a presentation.[3] But what if you were proactive and volunteered? Promotions, bonuses, and leadership positions come to those fearless few who can speak up in public. Obviously, Michael Bay's encounter with stage flight didn't hurt his directing career. However, quite possibly, it did reinforce his deepest fears about public speaking and will discourage him from taking to that kind of stage again. That being said, Bay is certainly not alone when it comes to stage *flight*. In fact, public speaking is the #1 fear in America.[4] We can talk about this fact all day long, but the real question should be: *Why* do we get so freaked out?

It turns out that *we're programmed to panic.*

Relatively Speaking

Three might be a crowd, but for our ancestors, it also meant not becoming a happy meal for a hungry pack of giant kangaroos.[5] Yes, carnivorous *kangaroos* used to prey on early humans. Humans also needed to fend off predatory hyenas, pythons, lions, tigers, and bears. Oh, my! Traveling in a pack reduced the chance of an attack. And you thought *your* commute was hairy.

The story goes something like this: Until about 12,000 years ago, our distant relatives were nomadic and spent a lot of time foraging for food.[6] They traveled in small groups, which was a necessity for survival. It allowed for some of the folks to look for food, while others kept an eye out for danger. The emphasis was on the tribe as a unit. And because these were the only people you knew on earth, it was imperative to keep one's individual tribe membership in good standing. The bottom line: If you were banished from your bunch, you became a kangaroo's lunch. To avoid this feast of fate, members adhered to social norms (not stand out), respected hierarchy (not stand out), and played nice with others (not stand out). You might see a pattern here. "Standing out" means the prospect of *rejection*. Rejection can lead to tribe *ejection*.

Oh, and forget about switching tribes if you're banished. Nothing doing. Evolution took care of that by equipping us with our very own "stranger danger" device. This funky feature saw anyone outside our group as a threat. So, if you did happen to run into another human, it's likely they would be highly suspicious of you—especially if you were traveling solo.

So what does this have to do with you and public speaking? After all, you probably aren't traveling in a pack, foraging for food, and fending off beasts. However, part of your brain still *thinks you are*. Okay, we'll explain. But before we get a-head (pun intended) of ourselves, you need to know something about your noggin.

Head Start

Our brains are remarkable in many ways, but there is one area that hasn't really evolved in 300 million years. It's appropriately called the *primitive brain*. How primitive is it? Steel yourself. Our own nerves, and the way they communicate, are comparable to the most ancient multi-organ animal on the planet: the jellyfish.[7] To put this in perspective, jellyfish have been around for, give or take, 700 million years. That's three times older than when the first dinosaurs roamed.[8]

The primitive brain's purpose is both singular and critical. To put it bluntly, it keeps us alive. It's the control center for our bodily functions, regulating breathing, heart rate, body temperature, digestion, elimination, reproduction, and balance.

The primitive brain also acts as our body's Department of Defense against outside threats. When we sense danger, it prepares us to *fight*, run (*flight*), or *freeze* (play dead).

Brain Trust

When the primitive brain detects fear it automatically switches us into fight, flight, or freeze mode. While in high alert, it also disconnects from the *thinking* part of the brain. This is actually a good thing, especially for those of us who have a hard time making decisions. Can you imagine bumping into a tiger and having your thoughts paralyze your progress?

"Hmm. Is that tiger looking at me or the mouthwatering antelope behind me?"

"Wait, is this a friendly tiger, or the one that ate my entire village last week?"

"Gee, I wish I had paid more attention in How-not-to-get-eaten-by-a-Tiger Class."

Okay, you get the idea. Although tiger run-ins are a rare scare, remember the primitive brain treats *all* threats (real or perceived) the *same* way. In other words, a modern version of a tiger attack just wears different stripes. For example, have you ever had a romantic crush on someone? They don't know you exist, but you know where they'll be at 3 o'clock on Tuesday. Yes, that kind. So what would happen if you ran into your crush unexpectedly in a supermarket aisle? Instantly, your primitive brain has you turning on your heels to get the heck out of there while your thinking brain has bolted to the bread section. At this point, the primitive brain is working in your favor because you can't remember your name, let alone know how to say something cool to your crush. What's the threat in this scenario? *Rejection*: "If I say something stupid, she/he will hate me forever!"

Although this all sounds like a pretty good deal (except for not getting a date), there is one drawback. Remember the primitive brain hasn't evolved much. Let's just say there haven't been a lot of new ideas flowing through it, like ever. Come to find out, evolution can be both industrious and totally lazy. In the case of the primitive brain, there was no need to "fix" something that wasn't broken. As far as evolution was concerned, the system was working, you're still alive, so why adapt beyond the basics?

We're about to sound really ungrateful here. So, don't get us wrong; the primitive brain does a great job of keeping us alive. However, it can't discern between the anxiety we feel when chased by a tiger and infinitely less dangerous fears like public speaking, closed spaces, and flying on an airplane.

Yes, for the primitive brain, *fear* is one size fits all. There is no internal "think tank" deciding if you are about to become a delicious tiger snack or, if you're a fearful flyer, boarding a plane to Pittsburgh on a snowy evening.

Fear of flying or, brace yourself, pteromerhanophobia is one of the top 10 fears for American adults.[9] Despite statistics showing commercial airline travel is overwhelmingly safer than all other ways we get around[10], this phobia keeps some of us permanently grounded. One would assume fearful fliers are afraid of the airplane crashing. Seems logical, right? If we're talking logic, however, many fearful fliers will tell you they *know* the fantastic safety record but *still* freak out. That's irrational behavior. So what else could be going on here? Scholars who study social phobias might tell you it *is* about survival, but perhaps not entirely how you would expect. A psychologist who treats anxious fliers recently revealed that two thirds of his clients are more terrified of freaking out and "alienating" other passengers than of *crashing*.[11] These same clients reported being scared of appearing "weird" to others. In other words, they were afraid of *rejection* from the group.

In this case, the anxiety is compounded. Not only does our primitive brain assume the crash position, it is terrified our nervous behavior will make us *stand out* in a group. And as our ancestors knew all too well, rejection could lead to tribe *ejection*. So, in a sense, "death" comes by way of *exclusion* rather than an *accident*.

Public Threat

Now that we know what the primitive brain can do, and what it fails at miserably, let's talk about how your brain reacts to public speaking.

First, public speaking means physically and figuratively standing out from a group. In doing so, our modern self gets sent danger signals from our ancestral past. It shouts:

"Hey, idiot, what are you doing? This group is going to reject you and your stupid speech. You want to die? Turn around slowly, then run!"

But wait, there's more. Lucky us, we also fear *strangers*. Though this might continue to benefit us in some respects, it's not so helpful when it comes to speaking in public. When looking into a crowd of unfamiliar, unsmiling faces, our evolutionary stranger danger device goes berserk. Now our ancestor self is screaming in our head:

"You don't know these humans. They may be dangerous. Don't trust them. And, by the way, they think your suit looks cheap. Run!"

So as these fear fireworks blast off in your head, what happens? Your primitive brain is in full-on survival mode. Biological buzzers are going off throughout your body. Your mouth is so dry you can't swallow. You suddenly feel light-headed and your face turns beet red. Your hands turn ice cold or your palms are slick with sweat. Oh, and of course, just when you need it most, your "thinking" brain is disconnected. Chances are you have experienced one or more of these reactions at some point. You're in good company. These are common physiological responses triggered by our primitive brain and what we typically refer to as *nerves*. Guess what? We all get them to some degree when it comes to public speaking. Sure, some people call them jitters, butterflies, apprehension, stage fright, or anxiety, or dress them up as "anticipation," but they all mean one thing: You're human.

In a later chapter, we'll explain why, despite our natural fears, when it comes to public speaking, audiences are *seldom* your enemy. In fact, we'll turn your primitive brain on its head and open up your mind to the notion that they actually *want* you to succeed. Take *that*, primitive brain!

In Be Twain

Samuel Clemens, better known by the pen name Mark Twain, famously said, "There are two types of speakers: those that are nervous and those that are liars."[12] In other words, we *all* get nervous. Twain himself gave more than 1,150 public speeches in his career[13] and knew what he was talking about. Frankly speaking, anyone who claims they can "cure" your public speaking nerves is talking out of both sides of his or her mouth. One public speaking book by a major publisher released in 2014 gives the impression it can do just that.[14] The title assures that you will *Never Be Nervous Again*. Let's be clear here: It's *impossible* to eliminate *all* nerves. Most jaw dropping is how the title seems to disempower the reader. Let's assume this author has a secret method for reversing at least 200,000 years of human evolution[15] and can make nerves disappear forever. After reading the book, inevitably a speaker will continue to get nervous. So who is to blame for this failure? After all, the book held all of the secrets to never being nervous again. It must be reader's fault when it doesn't work. That's really the only conclusion. The silliness of this "sale" confounds us. Though we applaud the writer for wanting to help people, it's like a cookbook author promising that if you follow his recipes, you will never be hungry again.

Why do we bring this up? Because we don't want you to buy into the false notion that there is magic cure to get rid of nerves or even that nerves are *bad*.

Make Nice With Your Nerves

As you have learned, nerves keep us alive. They keep you from having a picnic in the middle of the freeway or wandering down a dark alley at night. That can hardly be something you should be eager to get rid of. So, why not work with your nerves, instead of *against* them?

It's time to make nice with nature.

Let's go back to what happens to your body when you get nervous. It's usually the same symptoms (sweaty palms, the good old leg shake, or something equally annoying) and it drives you to distraction, right? You've tried to control nervous symptoms and even attempted to medicate them. Yet, they keep showing up every time you get anxious about something like public speaking. But let's stop here for a minute. We want you to consider something. If you *know* what your nervous symptoms are, and they occur *every time* you get nervous, then why are you so *surprised* every time they show up? It's like this: You know your hands get sweaty when you speak in public, yet when it happens you're thrown for a loop. Suddenly, all your focus is on your sweaty palms. It's time to start expecting the *expected*. Once you begin to *expect* and *accept* nerves when they do happen, you can start to acknowledge their primitive role and move past them.

White Out

We've had people tell us that despite understanding nerves are a natural part of public speaking, they still worry about going blank at some point during the speech. We call this a "White Out," where suddenly you're in some hazy fog and not sure which way to turn. In the next chapter, we'll talk about the power of visualization and the importance of positive self-talk. This should be helpful to avoid the

White Out scenario altogether. Generally speaking, another way to tackle this is with a lot of preparation and practice. Nothing beats it. You can't cram for a public speech. Well, not if you really want to shine. However, if you still find yourself in a White Out wipe out, we'll shed light on how to get you out of a fog.

First, don't assume the audience knows you're in one. Unless they wrote the speech, they have no idea what's supposed to come next. So, you're in charge, even when you feel like you're not. Second, *freeze*. We probably don't have to tell you that because you may already be there, but what we mean is don't fidget or start talking if you don't know what's going to come out. Most importantly, *do not* apologize or acknowledge your nerves! Again, the audience doesn't know you're experiencing technical difficulties. This is a tough thing to do, but it's critical.

Next, think of the last thing you said or remember saying. Then, turn whatever you said into a question for the audience. It can be rhetorical or if the situation is appropriate, you can actually pose a question. Asking questions is one of the most powerful ways you can engage an audience, while buying yourself time. Here's why: When you ask a question, even a rhetorical one, the audience goes into "answering" mode. They start thinking about the question, pulling focus away from you. This brief moment gives you time to catch your breath and get back on track. Let them ponder your question. No need to jump back in right away. If you have prepared and practiced, *hearing* the question out loud and taking this extra beat will likely lift the fog.

For example:

The last thing you remember is telling a story about a woman who found a wallet, turned it in, and received an unexpected reward. After that, you went into White Out mode. You might ask the audience any number of questions, including:

"So ask yourself: Would you have rewarded the woman? Aren't we expected to do the right thing?"

Or, "Have you ever found something valuable and considered keeping it?"

Or, "Have you ever lost something and it wasn't returned?"

Or, "Do you think the woman should have accepted the reward?"

Or, "What can we learn from this story?"

Or, "What does this story say about our society?"

Or, "How many of you have been in a similar situation?"

Get the point? There are numerous questions you can pose while you pull yourself out of the fog. It will not only buy you time, but will also engage your audience and they will assume it is part of your speech.

Physical Education

Public speaking is a *physical* activity and your body has much more of an influence on your mind than you may be aware of. This is a body, mind, and spirit effort. Runners, would you ever consider just hitting the path without stretching? All athletes know how important the mind-body connection is, as well as how to coax the best performance out of their bodies while avoiding injuries. It's really the same for speakers, or *should* be.

As we know already, public speaking causes all kinds of physiological changes. Anxiety causes our muscles to contract as the primitive brain is preparing us for fight, flight, or freeze, *so this is where you need to adapt where evolution hasn't.* Think about it. Standing with your muscles contracted and your jaw clenched tightly shut is not exactly the most relaxing way to give a speech. Not to mention that your body is sending a threat message to your mind. Other physical reactions to stress include: muscle tremors, twitches, difficulty breathing, rapid breathing, rapid heartbeat, chest pain, headaches, nausea/vomiting, vision problems, thirst, hunger, dizziness, excessive sweating, chills, weakness, fainting, and fatigue.[16]

Have you ever been really nervous and someone tells you to "just relax, calm down!" Did it work or did it just make you want to slap them? As if you wouldn't have "just relaxed" or "calmed down" if you could! Do people really think that, of all things, just relaxing is the thing we can't remember to do when we're nervous? If it were only that simple! The reason we can't just relax is because the anxiety is not just in our *minds*; our bodies have gone into fight or flight as well, so thinking "just relax" doesn't work. We need to help our body calm down so it can begin to tell the mind, "We are not in danger anymore and we *can* relax." Stretching, or moving your arms and legs, gives your nerves more space, reduces the tightness in your muscles, and allows your body to stay more fluid and flexible.

A bit of neuroscience for your reading enjoyment: The *vagus nerve* is the 10th cranial nerve that starts from our brain and connects to different parts of our body, creating a sort of communication highway. This is the reason we feel "butterflies in our stomach" when we are about to speak in public or our "heart breaks" when we get a heaping helping of "Let's just be friends." Interestingly enough, for our public speaking purposes, the communication lines between the brain and the body are disproportional. Twenty percent of the communication goes from the brain to the body and 80 percent travels from the body to the brain. This, by the way, explains why *telling* yourself to "relax" doesn't work. What happens in vagus stays in vagus. It's because the wiring sending that message only has 20-percent signal strength. So while you're telling yourself to relax, if your heart is beating fast and your breathing is shallow, your body is telling your mind that you are in danger. It would be like pitting a dial-up modem against high speed Internet. This means that changing our body posture can really influence the way we feel. Brain science says so!

Amy Cuddy, a social psychologist at Harvard Business School, studied exactly this and found that "Our nonverbals govern how we think and feel about ourselves. Our bodies change our minds."[17] She came up with the idea of *power posing,* which is adopting the physical stances associated with power, confidence, and winning: head held high, chest pumped out, and arms either lifted up in the Rocky Balboa pose or fists on the hips a la Wonder Woman. Cuddy suggests that everyone should spend two minutes in the power stance before heading into a job interview, giving a big speech, or competing in a sports activity. This power stance exercise can change your attitude right before a speech from nervous and scared to confident and powerful!

You need to make your body do your bidding, not the other way around. Be hands-on and wake it up. Although stretching won't eliminate your nerves, it will keep your body from tensing up, thus calming your mind. Adopting the power stance will tell your mind "we've got this." Between these two techniques, your brain is getting the message: I'm relaxed and confident. Both are necessary ingredients to ensure rocking your speech!

The Stupidest Public Speaking Advice and Why It Makes Us Crazy

If anyone has ever told you to "imagine your audience naked," it doesn't make them a bad person. It just makes them wrong, and perhaps a little creepy. Variations abound on this advice, sometimes allowing your audience to wear undergarments. Whatever the undress code, we can't think of anything *more* distracting than picturing an audience au naturel. We'll leave it at that.

Of course, the idea of this "clothing optional" approach is to somehow give you more confidence. With your audience reduced to their skivvies (or less), they are supposed to be scary-free. Maybe, but this advice emotionally "distances" you from the audience. Public speaking is about engaging a group of people, not pushing them away or fantasizing what they would look like nude. It's not *that* kind of engagement, people.

Our second-favorite-worst piece of advice is to "look above your audience" so that you don't have to catch anybody's eye. If the eyes are really the windows to the soul, the person who came up with this recommendation likely doesn't have one—a soul that is, not a window. Here's why: Humans look at each other. *Eye contact* builds connection and trust. Your eyes also communicate a heck of a lot of information. It's really that simple. If you aren't looking at your audience, you lose this extremely valuable communication tool. If you're still considering avoiding eye contact this way, try out this little experiment first:

The next time you meet up with friends or family, don't look them directly in the eyes. Instead, look *above* them. Act normally in every way, with the exception of giving them any direct eye contact. See how long it takes for someone to say, "Hey, dude, what's *wrong* with you?!" *Why?* Because it's really weird to look over someone's head when you're talking to him or her. It's the same thing with public speaking, but in this case there are a lot more people wondering what you find so interesting on the wall above them.

I Will Survive

We learned in this chapter why public speaking is somewhat of a head game. First, thanks to evolution, we're programmed to panic. When we feel threatened, our primitive brain goes into action, preparing us to fight, flight, or freeze. This causes physiological changes in our body, often identified as nerves. While all of this is happening, our "thinking" brain disconnects so we don't waste time contemplating our next move, which could cost us our life. This is also why your mind goes blank sometimes when you're nervous. Our ancestors also passed on another gift to us—and it wasn't just gab. As nomadic people, traveling in tribes instilled a terrifying fear of rejection and a fear of strangers. This manifests today in social phobias like the fear of flying and public speaking. Fundamentally, it's all about *survival*.

Understanding where our fears come from allows us to see that a) nerves are natural and b) we should work with, not against them. One fairly simple way to begin working with anxiety is to warm up your body before any public speech. Athletes do it to perform at their best and to avoid injuries. Public speaking is a physical activity, so we should do the same. Additionally, realizing that our bodies speak louder to our brains than our words, *saying*, "Relax, you've got this" to yourself before speaking in public, is not as powerful. Instead, before your speech, adopt a power stance for two minutes. Finally, we shared two of our favorite worst public speaking tips. Please don't picture your audience in undergarments or naked; that's just awkward. We also advise looking at, not *over* your audience. Both of these terrible tips defeat the basic purpose of public speaking: connecting with others to share an important message.

Try and Apply

Expect the Expected

Next time your nerves come on (and they will), the first thing to do is to *acknowledge* them. Don't try to fight your primitive brain. It's not smart and it doesn't have a heart so it won't respond to cajoling, reason, arguing, or tears. Instead, tell yourself:

"Of course, my palms are sweaty. They're always sweaty when I'm nervous. No surprise here."

This seems almost too simple, and to be honest, there's no mystery to it. However, by acknowledging that nerves are natural and allowing them to do their evolutionary job, you begin working your nerves, not the other way around. Suddenly, you will find that your nerves are no longer at the top of your mind. In fact, your "thinking brain" will come back online because you're, um, *thinking*.

Stretch Out

When you feel nervous, your body gets tense. This signals your brain that you are in danger, and you already know what happens when the body's Department of Defense gets activated: fight, flight, or freeze. Stretching allows the nerves to spread out and have more room; your body will thus feel more relaxed.

Adopt a Power Stance

Take two minutes before your speech and either stand like Rocky Balboa or Wonder Woman. These two power stances will tell your brain: We are confident, in control, and are going to knock this out of the park!

Key Notes

1. Expect the expected: Your brain is programmed to view public speaking as a threat so expect to get nervous. This will decrease the shock and help you focus on your speech.

2. Wipeouts: If your mind goes blank, ask a rhetorical question; it engages the audience and buys you time to get back on track.

3. Power posing: Right before your speech, do a superhero stance for two minutes. Your body will tell your mind, you got this!

Chapter 2

Hey, Are You Talking to Me?

You can speak well if your tongue can deliver the message of your heart.

—John Ford

Chapter Focus

How negative self-talk shuts you down.

Talk yourself into speaking.

Talk Me Through It

Whether you admit it or not, you talk to yourself. You're far from alone. Studies find that most of us use *self-directed speech* at least every four days, and many report self-chatter every hour. Researchers are also quick to add that talking to yourself doesn't mean you're crazy. In fact, self-directed speech can help us improve our memory, at least temporarily. Have you ever been walking out of the house and realized you don't know where you put your car keys? As you search the normal hiding spots and the truly irrational (Really? In your wife's jewelry box?), you are probably muttering to yourself the entire time. Turns out, if you are saying something like, "Key, keys, keys," you will find them faster. That's because saying the name of the object out loud helps you remember.[1] Another recent study suggests self-directed speech can be helpful when learning a new skill and meeting goals.[2] You can actually teach yourself by talking about it. Now, please don't take this as an opportunity to narrate everything you're doing 24/7. That's just annoying. However, we do want you to realize that when you say words out loud, you are hearing and processing them similar to when others speak to you. This idea becomes very important in relation to public speaking, as you'll find out shortly.

Use Your Inside Voice

There's another voice you hear sometimes, too: the one in your head. It's the voice that says things such as: "You aren't smart enough," "You look fat," or "You're going to mess this speech up and everyone is going to think you're stupid." Does any of this "inner" dialogue sound familiar? It sure does to us. In fact, all of us have this vicious vocal visitor at one time or another. It's our *inner critic*, sometimes referred to as the *anti-self.* Whereas "worry" is a natural response to stress and challenges, the inner critic twists everything so eloquently that we lose sense of our reality. It not only shoots down our confidence, it sometimes triggers mood swings and even leads to self-sabotage.[3] This is not your conscience by the way, or your moral guide. How can you tell the difference? Your conscience wants you to do the "right thing." The inner critic, on the other hand, is always punishing and destructive. It won't do anything to help you overcome an obstacle or make things easier. The inner critic is also so persuasive that it will convince you that the self-loathing you are experiencing is actually your idea. Its only job is to make you absolutely miserable. It probably started chattering at you the moment you found out you were giving a speech. We're going to help you shut this jerk up; but first, let's find out where this voice comes from and why it's so good at its bad job.

The Bully Inside: Where Does It Come From?

Your inner critic is an obnoxious bully. It's made even worse because you can't exactly cover your ears to shut out all the insults and jibes, as they're coming from *inside* your head. As we know, it never has a positive thing to say, nagging us to distraction and self-destruction. So why do we have it? Wait for it. Wait for it. It's all about *survival*. Yes, back to the primitive brain. Its main objective is to keep us away from being eaten or falling off a cliff. Its motto: better *safe* than sorry. The inner critic, like any bully, uses intimidation and persecution to make us do what it wants. So, it pulls out all the stops and pushes every one of your buttons to make sure you don't risk being mauled by a woolly mammoth. And herein lies the problem: Woolly mammoths have been extinct for 4,000 years.[4] Yet, our inner critic is still operating as if a herd of them will be waiting, disguised as members of the audience, when you get up to give your speech.

As you learned in Chapter 1, fight, flight, or freeze gets triggered because public speaking feels dangerous and threatening. Your inner critic is sounding the alarm. It shouts: "You're going to forget everything" or "People will think you're stupid." The goal is to thoroughly convince you not to speak in public. It will use every lowdown, nasty trick in the book to get its way because it has to. It believes that if you speak in public, people might reject and eject you from the group or, worse yet, attack you. This, of course, is something unpleasant to avoid.

Rick Hanson, a psychologist who has written on this phenomenon, explains, "There are two kinds of mistakes a person can make in life. They can either think there is a tiger in the bushes when there really isn't one, or they can think there is no tiger in the bushes, but there actually is one about to pounce. Mother Nature wants us to make the first mistake a thousand times over to avoid making that second mistake even once."[5] Can you understand now why your inner critic is so adamant and can get so mean and nasty? It believes it's saving your life.

Along with the inner critic, there is also the "outer" critic, and that one is all you. How often have you called yourself an "idiot" or "stupid" or "ugly" out loud? Remember that part about how self-directed talk helps us learn new skills and reach goals? Well, it works even when it's negative. Right. So not only is our inner critic hammering away at us, but also when we put ourselves down out loud, we are essentially teaching ourselves to be losers. It's no wonder so many of us are scared speechless!

But wait. You have a choice to listen to the inner critic or shout down its voice.

Accentuate the Positive, Eliminate the Negative

First, it's time to use self-directed talk for good, not evil. No more negative self-talk comes out of your mouth starting now. You've got a big speech coming up and desperate times calls for decisive measures. It's time to call in your reserves and clean up your trash talking. Nobody wants to hear it, including you. Look, it's not easy and we all do it. You're in the habit of doing it, so now make a habit of not doing it. Start catching and *correcting* yourself out loud. At this important time, do you really think teaching yourself how to be a loser is the best strategy to give an awesome speech? We don't either.

So what about that nasty inner critic? It seems to be getting louder the closer you are to speech day. Of course! It's gone into full-on panic mode. It thinks a woolly mammoth herd is about to trample you. If this were really the case, wouldn't you be yelling, pleading, cajoling, and insulting, too? Wouldn't you be doing everything you can to prevent someone from stepping up to give a speech in public that could result in a hairy disaster? Well, it's time to shout back. *We're serious.* Some people will tell you to "step away" from the voice or let it "flow" through you. We prefer the active versus the passive approach in this case. So let loose on it and shout back! Most likely it will get louder and more unbearable. But scream at it until it slinks away. And believe us, it will. Because the truth is, both the inner critic and bullies are cowards.

A bit of neuroscience again: The last 20 years of studying the brain has led to many important discoveries. A very interesting one, for our purposes, is that the old saying "You can't teach an old dog a new trick" is bogus! You *can* teach an old dog new tricks and actually rewire your brain. Not that we're calling you an old dog. But neuroscience has found that when you focus your attention on something new, your brain begins making new connections.[6] Focused attention plays a critical role in creating physical changes in the brain. The more purposeful and conscious your focus is, the more your brain, making different connections, begins to rewire itself. Out with old and in with the new!

A word of caution: With all the shouting, your family might think you've lost your mind altogether, so best to do this exercise when it's just you and your inner critic having it out. Oh, it will come back, in which case you can shout it down again or make a deal with it. You might say, "Look. Yes, I might listen to you and take your advice some day, but not today, not now, and not for this speech, so slither back into your cave." This is a little white lie. Of course, you want it to be gone forever. You can also thank it for trying to keep you safe, but as there aren't any woolly mammoths hanging around, you're good for now. Thanks but no thanks! Of course, feel free to use whatever "colorful" language it takes. With enough practice and focused attention, that old inner critic can turn into your biggest fan.

Now it's time to move the rest of your mind into action. Guess what? You can use words to do it, too!

Name It to Tame It

At some point in our lives we came to believe that if we pay attention to our anxiety it would get worse. Well, the exact opposite is true. Brain scientists have discovered that if you name your feelings, they actually dissipate or calm. They call it *name it to tame it*.[7] In other words, feelings are fluid and they come and go. The key is to stop fighting the anxiety and actually notice the sensations in your body and name them. For example, if you say, "Wow, my heart is beating fast and my chest feels tight. I'm feeling really nervous about giving my speech at work tomorrow," you could feel more relaxed about it. By actually naming what you are feeling, you might notice that the sensations will calm, even if just a little. And under these circumstances, every little bit counts! As your body calms, it signals the brain that you are not in danger, thus signaling the brain to stop releasing stress hormones to prep the body for fight, flight, or freeze.

That's another incredible way you can prepare your mind and body for the big day. Yes, we'll get to the part about practicing delivering your speech, but there's another kind of practice that can make your performance a success.

Imagery Is Just Like the Real Thing

Remember when we said that the primitive part of the brain wasn't so smart? Well, here's a way you can use that to your advantage. That part of the brain doesn't know the difference between real and imagined. Nope, we're not making this up. Try it. Imagine that you are about to give a speech. Do you notice yourself beginning to get nervous? Now, imagine that you are doing great and end up getting a standing ovation. Can you feel yourself calming down? *Imagining* yourself giving your speech in front of people and nailing it fools your brain into thinking that you have been successful at this before.

Additionally, studies show that imagining performing a skill will activate almost the exact same neural pathways as actually performing it, so that you can become better at something simply by imagining yourself doing it.[8] In other words, imagery can improve physical performance. This has been tested with athletes, musicians, and dancers. The groups that included imagery, in addition to practice, performed better than practice alone.

The imagining process is not just wishful thinking, by the way. It's a detailed mental rehearsal and, when combined with actual practicing, becomes a very powerful way to improve your public speaking.

Some people call this technique *visualization*. Whatever you call it, the key is to be specific with what you want to happen. Needless to say, keep your visualizations positive; if the inner critic steps in, tell it to go away and continue to imagine giving the best speech of your life. Again, this is different from just having a general attitude of "I'm going to do well." This is why you need to be thorough. The more details you can imagine, the more real it will seem to your mind and body. We recommend you do this exercise every single day including up to the moment of giving your speech.

Voices Carry

In this chapter, we've discussed how positive self-directed talk can improve our memory, teach us new skills, and achieve goals. We've also called out the inner critic inside all of our heads, that ancient bully who thinks it's saving us from certain death. Understanding these concepts allows us to overcome them.

We have ordered you to stop talking trash about yourself and use your voice to shout down the inner critic. This focused attention will make new connections in your brain, making it easier to quiet your inner critic and turn your adversary into your ally. You can also "name it to tame it"; in other words, voice your concerns out loud.

This should calm you down a bit. Finally, it's time to start imagining your feat. It's proven that when combined with preparation and physical practice, visualizing your success has a powerfully positive impact on your success as a public speaker.

Try and Apply

Combat the Inner Critic

There is a big difference from inter-directed talk and that inner critic that lives inside your head. Here's a way to begin to correct that bad habit: Start now by noticing how you speak to yourself. The first time you hear something negative, immediately stop and rephrase it into something positive, even if you don't believe it. The rest of the day, feel free to curse yourself out. Of course, we're kidding. The point is that the first time you catch yourself and rephrase it, you heighten your awareness to it and bullying yourself will no longer be okay. Be conscious and purposeful. Remember, the power is in the focus. Where you choose to put your attention changes your brain, how you see yourself, and interact in the world.

Noticing Tames the Beast

Emotions are like the waves in the ocean. Sometimes they feel like tsunamis and other times they feel like small ripples. Noticing what you feel and naming it will help calm the emotion down. If the thought of public speaking brings out a fast-beating heart or butterflies in your stomach, you are probably feeling anxious. By acknowledging the anxious feeling without judgment, you will help it calm. If it doesn't, notice the feeling with curiosity and ask yourself if it is okay to feel that emotion. Our bodies have a circuit breaker much like our homes' electrical system. The intensity of the emotion will come down—your nervous system is built that way—so challenge yourself to wait it out and notice how long it takes for the emotion to start its journey back to homeostasis.

Getting the Picture: How to Start Imagining!

Find a quiet, safe place. Sit in a chair with your legs planted firmly on the floor. Notice your feet on the floor and your butt on the seat. Now, notice your breathing. Listen to the sounds in the room. What do you hear? What do you smell? What do you feel? When you notice you are calm, begin to imagine giving your speech from beginning to end, moment by moment. Every so often, notice how you're feeling. Does your heart begin to beat a little faster? If so, ground yourself again, notice your feet on the floor, and butt in the chair. As you begin to calm down, keep going. Focus on breathing throughout the exercise and don't stop no matter what, even if you have to ground yourself 50 times while you're imagining giving your speech from start to finish.

Key Notes

1. Self-talk: Talking out loud makes learning a new skill easier and helps you remember.

2. Turn your inner critic into your biggest fan: Focusing your attention, consciously and purposefully, can help you change a negative thought into a positive one.

3. Name it to tame it: Don't be afraid of your emotions. Tune in and name the feelings you're experiencing; this will help them calm.

4. Visualize this: Imagery can improve physical performance, so imagining giving the best speech of your life will help you achieve it.

Chapter 3
Surprise, It's Not All About *You*

Make sure you have finished speaking before your audience has finished listening.

—Dorothy Sarnoff

Chapter Focus
Why speeches are always audience-centered.

Your audience is not your adversary.

We the People

Public speaking is not just about *you*. Though this might come as a shock, it's actually great news. If it were *just* about the speaker, an *audience* wouldn't be necessary. Without an audience, it's not "public" speaking. See how that works? Here's another way to look at it: You are giving this speech for a *reason* right? Chances are good it's not to tell people how gorgeous and smart you are. Although you might be both, you're speaking *at* a specific occasion *for* others and typically *not* about you. This shift in perspective immediately takes some pressure off of you. So, get out of your head (where negative thoughts lurk) and turn your attention to where it should be right now: *the audience.*

News flash: audiences are *alive*. Collectively and individually, an audience has dreams, emotions, hangups, desires, needs, and expectations. Though this may sound like a "duh" moment, think about what you've been told about "imagining your audience naked" or "looking above the audience" so you don't have to make direct eye contact. As we mentioned in Chapter 1, this advice encourages you to *distance* yourself from your listeners when you really should be doing everything you can to *engage* them. By detaching yourself from the audience, the experience becomes all about you, the speaker, increasing your anxiety and dehumanizing your audience. What if your minister never looks at the congregation during her sermon? Instead, she focuses her attention on the lighted red "exit" sign in the back sanctuary. Does she seem very engaged or interested in sharing a message? How does this make you feel?

So now that you understand you need to *connect* with an audience, where do you go from here? Well, first you have to find out as much as you can about them.

Population Control

Marketing professionals spend a lot of time studying *demographics*. Basically, demographics are quantifiable characteristics of a population. Commonly studied demographics include: age, gender, household income, and ethnicity. Based on demographics, marketers calculate how a group of consumers might respond to a given stimulus. The goal is to make sure whatever product, service, or idea a company is "selling" connects to consumers by meeting their *needs* and *expectations.*

In the same respect, the best way to *connect* with your audience is by *meeting or exceeding* their needs and expectations. This means thinking like a marketer and figuring out the demographics of your audience. Though this might sound hard, in reality, you do this on some level every single day. For instance, do you talk to fishing buddies the same way you chat with your grandmother? You probably don't. *Why?* You know your audiences and have tailored your style to meet their respective needs and expectations.

Although the audience you're preparing for right now is most likely larger, it's the same basic idea. Knowing your audience's demographics will guide you in both your preparation and performance. You'll have a better understanding of what words and tone to use, jokes to tell, how fast or loud to speak, what pop cultural references will work, and even what to wear.

On the Origin of Speeches

No offense, but you're self-centered. We all are. Personal self-interest is rooted in our basic need to survive. Does "survival of the fittest" sound familiar? Herbert Spencer coined the phrase after reading Charles Darwin's *On the Origin of Species.*[1] It basically means the biggest and baddest will survive. It really is all about survival! Have we mentioned that?

Our interest in self-interest didn't stop after the Bronze Age. "Relatively" speaking, life expectancy for our ancestors has only recently meant living past 50. Just 100 years ago in the United States, a man lived a mere 52 years on average. Women rocked it until age 57.[2] Our ancestors needed to be as self-centered as possible in order to stay alive each day, and we've inherited this trait. Part of the self-centeredness has to do with *What do I need to do to connect with people?* Remember: Rejection means tribe ejection. Audiences are also self-centered—collectively and as individuals. Yet, whether you're thinking of an audience as a whole or individually, they want to know one thing: *What's in it for me?* In other words, how are you going to meet my needs and expectations?

President Franklin Delano Roosevelt was arguably one of the greatest orators of the 20th century. He gave us some sound advice for meeting an audience's needs and expectations when he said, "Be sincere; be brief; be seated."[3] Roosevelt recognized that an audience expected a speaker to be truthful, passionate, and committed. He also understood an audience's limitations and that they were not there for your personal satisfaction.

So what are an audience's needs and expectations?

Know Your Audience and Speak Their Language

An audience has both *major* and *minor* needs and expectations. When looking at an audience as a group, we can identify two general or major needs and expectations. They are:

To suit the occasion: Is your speech appropriate for the event? Have you respected traditions, rituals, and the people involved?

To be prepared and perform: Depending on the occasion, an audience needs and expects to be enlightened, entertained, consoled, persuaded, or inspired in the most *efficient* way. The audience is self-centered. They are there for themselves, not *you*.

However, we know audiences are made up of individuals and every individual has his or her own needs and expectations. For our purposes, let's call these minor needs and expectations. An audience's minor needs and expectations can be *physiological,* like having to use the restroom, needing an aspirin, or daydreaming of the roast beef dinner they'll enjoy when they get home. They can also be *emotional,* like wishing you will acknowledge their dedication to the company in front of everyone—or hoping you *won't*.

Later on, we'll guide you through the creative process of writing your speech, how to practice and memorize, and finally, make it all sound conversational and appropriate for your particular situation.

Play in the Majors

A common mistake made in the "performance" aspect of public speaking is playing to the *minor* needs and expectations to the detriment of the major ones. We call this *recruiting audience members*. To better understand this concept, let's first look at two common ways speakers relate to an audience.

One group of speakers ignore the audience altogether or imagine them in unimaginable scenarios (for example, naked). Ignoring your audience altogether makes for a very lopsided and awkward experience. Essentially, it becomes speaker-centered and the audience is disposable. In this scenario, a speaker can come off as very stiff and robotic. Imagine you are giving your speech, say something witty, and the audience laughs, but you don't pause. Instead, you speak over the laughter and move on to your next point. By the time the audience gets quiet and starts to listen again, they're lost and you don't get to bask in their appreciation of your wittiness.

On the other side of the spectrum, many speakers read into every move and sound coming from the audience. This is often because they're trying to meet or exceed the *minor* needs and expectations of individual audience members. In other words, they are trying to recruit individual audience members (to like them) by guessing what their reactions are communicating. This approach might be tempting, but it is a slippery slope that can lead to overcompensation and/or wandering off your prepared path. We are certainly not advising you to ignore the commonsense feedback an audience gives you (for example, applause, laughter, sighing, head nodding, strong eye contact, crying). These are all signs the audience is engaged and/or understanding your speech. However, to paraphrase an old adage, "You can please some of the people some of the time, and some of the people all of the time, but you can't please all of the people all of the time."[4] So we caution you from putting too much stock into what individuals might be communicating through physical or even audible reactions.

To illustrate this point, let's say you've done your demographic homework and prepared your speech on the general characteristics of your audience. Yet, once you're up and speaking, instead of focusing on what you know, you start trying to guess what individuals need and want and then react accordingly.

It might look something like this: You're giving a speech and a young couple appears to be very unhappy with what you're saying, how you're saying it, or both. The guy seems really frustrated. His female companion is staring angrily up at the ceiling. Obviously, you've done or said something wrong. You must really be messing up! How can you fix this? Suddenly, you can't remember what you were saying. Of course, you have no way of knowing that a minute earlier, the guy got a text message from his ex-girlfriend. Now a big fight is brewing. Unless you're the ex-girlfriend, this has nothing to do with you. Yet, you *reacted* to it like it had *everything* to do with you. Needless to say, it negatively affected your performance. As we mentioned earlier, minor needs and expectations can be physiological, too. If someone pulled an all-nighter, they might look half-asleep. You have no way of knowing who is hungry, has to go to the bathroom, is flunking out of math, is not feeling well, just got laid off, is pregnant, or any number of influences that might send messages you are bound to misread and make wrong assumptions about.

Yes, there are also times when audience members give you really amazing feedback. Enjoy that, but don't let it make or break your performance, either. If that friendly woman in the front row gets up and leaves, what do you do then? You were banking on her friendly smile to get you through the speech. Now, not only are you absolutely sure she *hates* your speech, you were counting on her to give you reassurance. How could you know she has allergies and was afraid her sneezing would distract you? She's now standing in the hall, but listening and still enjoying your speech.

So obviously, ignoring the audience entirely is not a great choice, but focusing on all the minor needs and expectations of individual members of an audience, and making automatic assumptions based on their behavior, is asking for trouble. Our advice is to be aware of and adapt to common sense audience reactions, but your goal is to play in the majors and do your best to forget the rest.

Speaking With the Enemy

When it comes to public speaking, most of us automatically make the audience the adversary. That's actually a pretty natural response. After all, doesn't our society rate and rank almost everything? The fact is we judge others, too. But public speaking is an entirely different thing. This kind of judgment feels like a death sentence. But wait. You've assumed the audience is your enemy. This cannot be further from the truth. However, blame it on your primitive brain. That's right, it's hard at work convincing you these strange faces are dangerous and the familiar ones will kick you out of the tribe if you mess up. Again, it's time to adapt where evolution hasn't helped us. In this case, it just means understanding that a "modern" audience is almost always on your side. That's right, your audience *wants* you to do well. Yes, we know this sounds too simple and far too good to be true, but there are three very good reasons why this is actually the case.

First, we've all been in your place and the fear of messing up is palpable. Have you ever been listening to a speaker and suddenly he loses his train of thought? He stands there for several uncomfortable seconds. No one in the room is breathing, but there seems to be a collective effort to *will* the speaker to find his place again and continue. Honestly, no one wants to see a speaker fail—well, unless it's in politics. When a speaker struggles, we feel for him. When a speaker gets back on track, there is often a sigh of relief, audible words of encouragement, nervous laughter, or even applause. Why? We can truly imagine how awful it must be.

The second reason has to do with, once again, survival of our species. As much as you don't want to be shunned or disliked by the audience, the audience doesn't want to be shunned or disliked by you! Because connecting with the speaker, to each of their primitive brains, increases their chances of survival as the smart speaker surely knows how to ward off the approaching tiger! Connecting with the speaker feels safe because the audience views *you* as the authority.

The third reason goes back to the *What's in it for me?* question. They came to listen to you because they believed they would get something out of it. If they are there, it's because they want to be. If they were forced to be there, someone thought they would benefit from your speech. So, even the forced bunch is looking to connect because they *have* to be there. Better to be entertained than to be bored on top of forced. Given that premise, if you engage an audience that already wants to engage with you, it's a win-win. An audience can get restless when they're not engaged and if their major needs and expectations aren't being met. Think about the worst speech you've ever endured. What was it about? Chances are good that you can't remember what it was about because the speaker was so boring you had to keep jabbing a pen into your hand to stay awake.

Okay, now try to recall the most amazing speech you've ever heard. Both the speaker and her message were awesome. You felt totally invigorated when she finished and time seemed to fly by.

So, if you had to hear one of those speeches again, which one would you choose? We're going to assume you'd choose the amazing speech. That's because no one, including your audience, wants to be lulled to sleep by a tedious talker. Your audience isn't thinking, "Gosh, I hope this speaker is tedious and uninteresting today." It's completely the opposite. An audience is on your side. They are rooting for you—if only because they don't want to keep stabbing pens into their hands.

Connection Equals Direction

Understanding the audience wants you to succeed takes the pressure off and can decrease your anxiety. Connecting with them becomes easier because you know that they want to engage with you. However, as the speech giver, it is your job to find ways to relate to your audience. Researching your audiences' demographics will point you in the right direction. So, if you are giving a sales pep talk, you know that your audience is full of salespeople. Sales people have to sell a product, so most people who go into that field are outgoing extroverts and find it easy to talk to people. In this case, a lively and interactive speech will be a win out of the gate. Give it pep! If you're presenting or accepting an award, humor goes a long way on an extra long night. When presenting a new product your company has just launched, everyone is going to be interested in what it's all about, so be enthusiastic, too! The more passion you demonstrate when describing it, the more passion they will feel too. Mood is contagious! However, make it genuine. So if you're not really that jazzed about the new product, find at least one thing that you can get behind and funnel that passion into the entire product. This passion will propel your entire presentation and make an authentic connection with the audience.

Try and Apply

Remember, It Is Not About You

Remembering that public speaking is more about what you are talking about and less about you, the person giving the speech, is very helpful. Think back to the last time you went to hear someone talk. Unless it was a celebrity, chances are you could pretty much care less about the person giving the speech and were really there to hear the information they promised to impart. Knowing this takes some of the pressure off of you and puts the focus where it should be, on the information itself.

Speaking the Same Language

Spend some time researching the population you will be speaking to:

- Who are they?
- Why are they there?
- What do they want to learn from it?
- How can you best deliver that?

Needs and Expectations

Focus on *major* audience needs when developing your speech. Don't take *minor* audience needs personally and don't make assumptions on the behavior of your individual audience members.

The Audience Is Not Your Adversary

Remember that the audience wants you to succeed. It is uncomfortable and awkward to see the speaker struggling up there. They see you as the expert and want you to like them. *And* it is truly all about them; they want to be entertained. So as long as you are doing that, they will love you!

Key Notes

1. You are the least of their worries: Remember that public speaking is not about you. The audience is more interested in the information than the giver of the information.

2. Needs and expectations: Spending time doing research on your audience's demographics will help you tailor your speech to best meet their needs and expectations.

3. Focus on the broad picture: Don't get stuck on what individual audience members are doing and keep your focus on the room as a whole.

4. The audience is not the enemy: They want you to succeed. They view you as the authority and want you to like them as much as you want them to like you.

Chapter 4
Tell Me a Story

To be a person is to have a story to tell.

—Isak Dinesen

Chapter Focus
The secret power of stories.

How to spin a great yarn.

So What's the Story?

Telling stories isn't a modern invention. Long before humans had a written language, we were swapping them. Our ability to create and share stories is one of the few truly universal human traits, found in all cultures throughout history and serves an essential purpose; they help us understand the world and our place in it. Storytelling helps us educate[1], entertain, preserve history, pass on traditions, show affiliations, and reinforce social mores. You can learn a lot about a society's belief system by looking at its fairy tales, parables, proverbs, legends, myths, jokes, and even nursery rhymes.

Additionally, many stories throughout history, regardless of culture or time, share common structural or literary devices. The late American scholar Joseph Campbell believed all stories everywhere share a fundamental structure, what he called a monomyth, the *hero's journey*.[2] Campbell identified several steps our "hero" archetype takes along a journey including: leaving home, overcoming great challenges, and eventually returning home having been endowed with special wisdom or powers. Campbell's work has influenced artists and writers around the world, including *Star Wars* maestro George Lucas.[3]

What's also fascinating about the human history of storytelling is that similar *motifs* (recurring objects or ideas in a narrative) pop up in all major cultures throughout the world, suggesting the same origin.[4] The "great flood" narrative is a prime example. Though many Christians and Jews might have heard of the biblical story of Noah and his ark[5], strikingly similar stories are found all over the world in different faiths and even centuries before Noah's adventures were chronicled in the Book of Genesis. This knowledge becomes especially important if you're considering incorporating stories into speeches because it illustrates how common themes might resonate and, therefore, connect with your audience organically. We'll explore this idea later in the chapter when we talk about "universal themes," but first, what's *your* story?

A Storied Life

Has anyone ever told you that your life could be a movie or make a great reality show? This observation usually follows one of your especially zany, dramatic events or escapades. On the other hand, maybe you don't think your life is all that exciting. If this is the case, time to reconsider. Every up and down of daily life is a story disguised as a victory, deed, or disaster. Take a closer look because you don't want to miss out on one of the most effective strategies you can use in a speech. There are many reasons why this is true. The first is that you are a natural-born storyteller. You think and communicate in stories all day long. In fact, personal stories and gossip fill 65 percent of our conversations.[6] This means your audience will be all ears for your story, too! Yet, our attention to stories goes deeper than that.

Intellectual Properties

When it comes to public speaking, an audience is far more likely to remember a powerful story over "facts and figures" long after the speech is over. It's not only because we're used to telling and listening to them. Humans are hardwired to hear them. When someone tells us a story, our brain immediately starts working to connect it with our own experiences. As we search through our intellectual inventory, the *insular cortex* in our brain kicks in, cuing us to identify with emotional elements of the story.[7] This means that whether they are used to entertain, inform, or persuade, stories are effective because they appeal directly to our emotions and sense of empathy.[8] This is great news for public speakers. It's like moving into an apartment that's already cable ready. Your audience is already hooked up and ready for you to flip the proverbial switch.

Universal Remote

What supercharges stories in speeches and in literature are *universal themes*. As we mentioned at the beginning of the chapter, these are central ideas that are found across the world, throughout time, and in almost every story ever told. These tales as old as time include: human (man or woman) against nature, human (man or woman) against self, human (man or woman) against society, human (man or woman) against human (man or woman), coming of age, eternal love, love lost, triumph over great odds, sacrifice brings rewards, crime doesn't pay, and the importance of family. These types of themes drive the narrative, but are so ingrained in our psyche that we might not even be conscious of them. These are akin to, but not the same as, motifs. The "great flood" motif is a structural device used to illustrate a universal theme. In this case, it could be "man against nature," "triumph over great odds," or a number of others depending on the culture, religion, and respective worldview.

Telling stories with popular universal themes is one of the most effective ways to introduce an audience to new ideas and concepts. George Lucas isn't the only guy in Hollywood who takes full advantage of this benefit. It's a big reason period pieces (past or present settings) work so beautifully even though we live in the present. Take the 2006 Oscar-nominated film *Apocalypto*. It's set in 1511, in pre-Columbian Petén, Guatemala, around the end of the Mayan civilization. The story follows a young Mesoamerican tribesman named Jaguar Paw (played by Rudy Youngblood) on an epic quest to rescue his family after their village is destroyed and he's captured.[9] All the dialogue is in the Yucatec Maya language. It might surprise you to learn that not very many Americans speak or understand Yucatec. In fact, everything about the movie seems completely removed from our cultural experience. So how can an audience have zero connection to Jaguar Paw's culture or world-view at the beginning of the movie, but quickly become completely invested in his well-being? Stated another way, how is it possible we become empathetic to his specific situation? First, the hero's journey as the fundamental structure is instantly recognizable and familiar. However, the emotional connection would never have been possible without the framework of universal themes. *Apocalypto* overflows with universal themes like: man vs. nature, man vs. society, man overcoming great obstacles, love and the importance of family. In other words, universal themes opened the door and allowed us to step into the world (and shoes) of someone who we deemed as completely different.

You can craft the same experience for your audience. If you need your audience to identify or empathize with a person, place, or thing that is completely foreign to them, do it with a universal theme as a backdrop. Then create a very specific world, and feel the connections happen.

The Underdog Effect

There is another archetype we have to tell you about because it is scientifically proven to be effective with almost all audiences; it's a *psychological* phenomenon. We're talking about the *underdog*. One of the most famous "underdog" stories is that of David and Goliath.[10] The story, found in the Bible's Books of Samuel, chronicles the battle between a giant Philistine warrior, Goliath, who is felled by a much smaller David, a future king of Israel and Judah.

The biggest surprise, perhaps, is that the underdog phenomenon doesn't have to have David winning. We might like our winners, but we *love* our losers. That is, we root for the underdog—even when they lose. Remember first hearing about the Butler University Bulldogs a few years ago? Although the small Indiana school now sports a solid reputation for men's basketball, back in 2010, not so much. In what was touted as a "Cinderella story," the Bulldogs charged through the NCAA Tournament that year to take on the powerhouse Duke University Blue Devil's for the National Championship. Duke overshadowed Butler University in almost every way. Yet, here was Butler on the finals court duking it out. In the end, Butler missed a game-winning shot at the buzzer and Duke took the title. But it almost didn't matter. The Bulldogs had won millions of fans and goodwill from media outlets around the world. The *New York Post* even called the Bulldog's loss "triumphant."[11]

Research has also shown that U.S. Americans are 80 percent more likely to champion the underdog in almost every kind of situation, be it in sports, politics, entertainment, academics, or business.[12] So what's going on here? Are we *that* nice? Maybe, but scholars say it all might come down to our respect for justice and fairness. We also tend to evaluate an underdog's characteristics differently than the top dogs. We see the underdog in a more positive light, one who is at an unfair advantage, overcoming greater obstacles. Finally, we see ourselves in the underdog. We have all struggled at some point. Maybe you've been bullied or faced hardship or challenges. Remember that mean inner critic of yours? Ultimately, we all know what it's like to face Goliath, so we relate to the underdog and cheer them on.[13]

Obviously, the underdog archetype won't work for every speech, but don't forget about it for the future. It's one of the most effective storytelling devices you can use. Okay, now let's move on to how to best use your stories in your speech.

Story Lines

There are several kinds of storytelling approaches you can use in a speech ensuring your audience gets the message. One of the most popular and effective is an *analogy*, which compares a familiar idea with one that may be unfamiliar to your audience. As former presidential speechwriter John Pollack explains, "The most effective analogies, comparisons that resonate emotionally, use the familiar to illuminate the strange."[14] The intent of analogies is to show how two different ideas actually share traits, which can serve as "shorthand" for speakers and audience. For example, one widely used and effective analogy is the "domino effect." It's a quick way to cut through a lengthy explanation about chain reactions. Arguably, your audience will also have a stronger visceral response to "falling dominos" over a description like "one event setting off a sequence of events."

Analogies are also useful when you need to illustrate the size of an object or want an audience to grasp a number so large that it risks becoming abstract for them and, therefore, meaningless. When talking about size, we're sure you've heard everything from homes to countries described in terms of how many "football fields." Citrus fruit is very popular in medical parlance: "When the vet removed Goldie's tumor, it was the size of a grapefruit." Numbers and statistics, just like sizes, can also be so abstract they become impersonal. If a speaker feels this is a risk, she might bring those numbers closer to home. For instance, she could take a number and "translate" it through an analogy like this: "That's roughly five times the number of students who go to this college" or "Statistically, that means half the people in this room will experience some level of hearing loss before turning 50."

Some analogies are more "figures of speech" comparing two unlike things to make your point more vivid for an audience. For instance, *similes* are comparisons that are linked by the words "like" or "as" where the traits of one thing *resemble* the traits of another. Commonly used similes are "as cute as a button" and "like two peas in a pod." These figures of speech can be especially useful when introducing new technical, scientific, or other complex information to an audience by comparing it with something already familiar to them. For example, if you're giving a speech on cells, you might say: "A cell is like a hotel. The nucleus is like the hotel manager, controlling what happens in the cell. The cell membrane, just like a hotel security officer, controls the perimeter."

Similar to similes are *metaphors*, which have the same basic function, but in this case, the traits of one thing symbolically *replace* that of another. If you've ever said something like "He was a breath of fresh air," "Her room is a pigsty," or "You are the sunshine of my life," you've made a metaphor. Usually, if you use a metaphor, you won't use a simile and vice versa. This doesn't mean it can't be done, it just means you have to be a wordsmith or Winston Churchill. The late British prime minister used both (simile followed by a metaphor) describing his first encounter with President Franklin Roosevelt. Churchill noted, "Meeting [FDR] was like opening your first bottle of champagne; knowing him was drinking it."[15]

Another storytelling technique is the use of *testimonials*. These are first-person accounts from someone with a direct connection to the subject matter like an expert (for example, scientist, professor, or top business professional) or a layperson. Both kinds of testimonials can be equally effective, but for different reasons. Citing an expert who believes the way you do, adds to your topic's credibility. But a layperson who witnessed or experienced something first-hand can be just as convincing (for example, cancer survivor, foster mother) because it's difficult to challenge someone's feelings. Just like analogies, testimonials can also be especially useful to help statistics or big numbers "land" with your audience. For instance, let's say you have to talk about how 50 million U.S. Americans suffer from neurological disorders. Although that number is striking, it doesn't offer much in the way of emotional impact. However, what if you followed it up with an example of someone battling a neurological disorder, like Muhammad Ali, or someone who isn't famous at all? Hearing "testimony" from someone struggling with a neurological disorder connects an audience with a number, which can be too abstract to absorb intellectually and certainly doesn't have the same emotional appeal.

Another storytelling option is to use an *anecdote* to illustrate a point. These are short stories from the speaker's life or the life of someone else (usually someone famous). They can be witty, poetic, poignant, or serious. Here's an example of a personal anecdote, illustrating how the speaker learned about his own resilience.

"My family used to go to the same resort every summer. One of my earliest memories is splashing around in the pool. I remember hanging on the side because I couldn't swim yet. My dad was sitting not too far away. It was pretty crowded so I kept moving myself closer to the deep end. Suddenly, I slipped off the ledge and I started sinking down. And down. And down. It was weird because I didn't panic. When my feet touched the bottom, I pushed myself up to the surface, caught a breath and then sank down again. This went on and on. Each time I hit the bottom, I used my feet to push myself back up. Finally, my dad reached down and pulled me out of the water. I've never forgotten it."

Short stories about famous people always make interesting anecdotes, especially if they are not widely known. Many years ago, a friend told us an anecdote about famous opera singer Jessye Norman. It goes like this:

"It was 9:45 a.m. and the production crew in the San Antonio Convention Center was ready to pack it in. The international opera star Jessye Norman was due in 15 minutes to rehearse for a special performance that afternoon. The crew had worked with 'divas' before, and a few had heard she was definitely of that persuasion. They were convinced she wouldn't arrive on time for rehearsal, let alone the actual performance. But 10 a.m. on the dot, Ms. Norman strode in, regally, still wearing dramatic stage makeup. You see, hours earlier, she had performed a full opera and after the last curtain call, she had walked off the New York stage without removing her makeup. She changed clothes in midstride. Then she sped to the airport and flew all night to San Antonio. Later, after the crew learned this, one of the producers thanked her for making it to the rehearsal on time. Ms. Norman simply smiled and said graciously, 'I gave you my word.'"

In the next section, you'll see how these anecdotes could work in a speech.

Heads and Tales

One of the best places to tell a story (especially a really funny or dramatic one) is at the beginning of your speech as an attention-getter. We know audiences love stories and are wired to connect with them, so it's a no-brainer to use a story to connect with your audience immediately and naturally! Of course, you can pepper the middle of your speech as needed with storytelling devices like analogies, similes, metaphors, and testimonials anytime you need to downsize a monster number or statistic or introduce new information to your audience. Finally, you can end your speech with a story. This is usually the perfect choice if you start your speech with one because you then "book end" your speech with the same story. You don't say the same exact thing, of course, but should either refer to it, or finish it. So for example, if we started our speech with the personal anecdote about the kid almost drowning in a pool, we could conclude our speech by using it again to make a point:

"I'll never forget that summer when I almost drowned. I learned three things that day. First, stick close to family. Second, watch that you don't wander too far into the deep end. Finally, if and when I ever 'hit bottom,' I will land on my feet and push myself up to the surface again. And I know you can too."

Or, if we used the Jessye Norman anecdote to kick off our talk, we could wrap it up this way:

"The crew and producers were expecting a 'diva' that morning in San Antonio. And when opera star Jessye Norman showed up, they got one. The word 'diva' is tossed around a lot these days and if you call yourself a diva you probably aren't one. Because when you look up the real definition of diva, it means to be 'celebrated.' It's not a self-ascribed title; it's earned. So, if you want to be a real diva, act like one. Work hard, be a pro, and above all, keep your promises."

Beware of Tall Tales

If you've ever been on the wrong end of a nasty rumor, you know that stories can harm. Fabrications among friends can be an awful experience, but being untruthful as a public speaker may have serious personal and professional consequences. For starters, if you tell a tall tale as truth, you're asking for big trouble. This might sound overly dramatic (even for the chapter on storytelling), but as a speaker, you have a sacred contract with your audience to be honest. You can make mistakes, but they should be honest ones.

This doesn't mean you can't add flourishes, embellish for theatrical effect, or even reorder a time line a bit to create a compelling story. It does mean that you have to remember that telling a story in public is different from sharing one in casual or personal conversation. The stakes are higher and so are the consequences.

Greg Mortenson's story about getting lost in Pakistan while mountain climbing and being nursed back to health by strangers is the basis for a best-selling 2007 book, *Three Cups of Tea*.[16] He promised his rescuers he would build a school to thank them for their kindness. The publicity from his book and subsequent speaking tours persuaded thousands of Americans, including schoolchildren, to donate millions of dollars to a charity he established to build not one, but hundreds of schools in central Asia. But in 2010, allegations began to surface that Mortenson had fabricated the story told in *Three Cups of Tea* and that he was using his charity as a "personal ATM." Soon, Mortenson's credibility began to unspool. He later confessed the stories in *Three Cups of Tea* were amalgamations of several trips during a number of years and reimbursed the charity for $1 million.[17] Mortenson lost a tremendous amount of credibility as a speaker because he broke a sacred contract with his audience.

Tale of Two Stories

Given that storytelling is a universal human trait *and* we are wired to process and remember stories, there's a pretty good case for you using a story or two in your speech. But where do you start?

Many new speakers are tempted to tell a story that has nothing to do with their speech, just because they know it or think it's amusing or interesting. This is a big waste of time and risks confusing your audience. Stories are meant to support the message of your speech, not detract from or work against it. Additionally, beginning public speakers often have trouble discerning which of their personal stories work well for speeches. This is why we always have them start with the underdog story. Remember how powerful that archetype is? One of the reasons it resonates is because we've all felt like the underdog at some time in our lives. We asked our student Chad to write down a time in his life when he felt like an underdog. Here's what he wrote down and shared with us.

"When I was 15, I started wrestling. When I showed up for my first tournament, there weren't any other kids in my weight class. So, they bumped me up to the next weight class. All the boys, there were seven of them, were 16 and were bigger than me. Everybody, even my coach, kind of counted me out before I even started. And it was hard. Those guys were way heavier than me. But I ended up beating three of them and took fourth place."

It's a classic underdog story. Chad was pinned underneath the general consensus that he was going to lose, even before his first match. The story is also full of universal themes. Along with the underdog, we identified "triumph over great odds," "man against man," and "coming of age." So next, we asked Chad how he felt about placing fourth in his adopted weight class. He said, "Great!" This was interesting to us because most people wouldn't consider coming in fourth place so "great." This gave us an idea for one of the ways he could use this story in a speech. Let's say Chad is doing a speech on the importance of determination or even America's obsession with winning, he could tell the story like this:

"I'm 15 years old. I am trying to move, but this kid is 16 and has about 10 pounds on me. Did I mention that it's my first wrestling meet? Or that when I showed up this morning, there were no other guys in my weight class, so they bumped me up to compete with the brutes? I'm trying to put on a game face, but everybody is telling me not to be too disappointed when I lose. In the end, out of seven guys, I came in fourth. In our society, we put a lot of weight into winning. If we're not #1, well, we're nothing. But what my 15-year-old self can tell you is this: That afternoon, so many years ago, when I was pinned underneath this older kid, knowing full well I was seconds away from a loss, I was smiling like a goofball because I had tried my best. And I don't care what anybody else thinks, because I know this for a fact: If you try your best, a fourth place can feel just like first."

There are other ways Chad can use this story in a speech. It would only mean emphasizing a different point or setting a different tone, but that's the cool thing about stories: They can illustrate so many truths about life. Can you come up with any other lessons Chad could have learned from this experience?

Do you have a similar story? Even if doesn't sound like Chad's, we're pretty sure you've felt like an underdog at some point in your life. Write it down. It doesn't have to be terribly long, but should have details like: who, what, when, where, and why. Then think of different ways you can use it to illustrate a point, lesson, moral, or belief.

Additionally, we encourage you to rethink the moments in your life that mattered and begin jotting them down. As a burgeoning public speaker, it would be smart to start keeping an inventory of stories you can pull out for different occasions. And remember: One story can usually be interpreted in several ways!

Having the Last Word

In this chapter we learned that storytelling is a uniquely human trait. Storytelling is how we make sense of the world and we've been telling them for ages. Humans are also wired to process and remember stories. This makes storytelling a powerful device in public speaking and we encourage you to include a story or two in your speech. Remember how universal themes can open the door for audiences to learn about and embrace new people, places, and things. You can use a story at the very beginning of your speech, in the middle to illustrate a point (especially to bring a human face to big numbers), and also at the end. If you use a story at the end, it's best to refer back to the same one you used in the beginning, as it creates a cleaner overall effect. Most importantly, remember you have a sacred contract with your audience to tell the truth; if this is broken, your credibility and your message are, too.

We also want you to get into the habit of listening to great storytellers. Here are a few places on the Internet where you'll find them:

TheMoth.org.

ThisAmericanLife.org.

TheMemoryPalace.us.

TheStory.org.

RadioDiaries.org.

There's also a really amazing Website where you can record your own stories and listen to people share their tales of loss and triumph. It's called StoryCorps.org.

Try and Apply

Listen to the Story

Storytelling is a universal human trait. Begin to notice how many times you engage in this storytelling ritual. It's probably more than you have ever noticed! The good news is that you have been practicing "speechwriting" without even trying. Now notice how many times you are listening to your friend, family member, coworker, neighbor—the list goes on and on—tell *you* a story. Notice what kind of stories grabbed your attention most. Did they fall into one of the universal themes?

- Human against nature.
- Human against self.
- Human against society.
- Human against human.
- Coming of age.
- Eternal love.
- Love lost.
- Triumph over great odds.
- Sacrifice brings rewards.
- Crime doesn't pay.
- Importance of family.

Observing this will give you a good start when you begin to prepare your speech.

Points to Consider as You Put Your Story Together

1. Have a beginning, middle, and end. This sounds like another "duh" moment, but it gives you a natural outline to start working from.

2. Have a clear protagonist and vibrant characters. Boring characters are just that.

3. You don't need to tell your story in chronological order. You can start at the end and work backward if that provides a more surprising result for your audience.

4. Avoid making yourself the "hero" if possible. Hint: Even if it's not a classic underdog story, your protagonist needs to be either likeable or wildly interesting.

5. Have an obstacle or obstacles your protagonist (or you) needs to overcome. What is the lesson to be learned?

6. Use vivid language!

7. Remember to write it to be *said*, not to be *read*. Tell a story; don't read an essay (more on this in Chapter 6).

8. Use humor and/or drama to create tension. A little self-deprecating humor is effective in making you and your plight relatable to your audience. Too much self-deprecation is a turnoff.

9. Share a "short story." In other words, a story's function is to support your point, not be it.

10. Be honest and accurate. Rearranging a story can be helpful for storytelling purposes, but make sure you keep your credibility contract with your audience!

11. Practice, practice, practice. Try timing your story and also telling it to a friend or family member. After you're finished, ask them to repeat the story back to you. If they have

difficulty doing so, this could be a big clue that you need to rework the story. Remember: You know the story, other people don't. You might have to do a bit more explaining in some parts and less in others, depending on your audience.

Key Notes

1. We are natural storytellers: The brain is hardwired to find a common ground and relatable themes in any story.

2. Universal themes: Supercharge your speech by writing it using a universal theme to engage your audience.

3. Storytelling isn't random: Use one of the universal storytelling techniques as the foundation for your speech.

4. The unspoken oath: The audience expects you to be honest. You can stretch the truth, but don't jump off the tracks.

Chapter 5

Use What You Know
to Steal the Show

They may forget what you said, but they will never forget how you made them feel.

—Carl W. Buechner

<u>Chapter Focus</u>
The roles of self-concept in public speaking.
What you see is what you get.

Labels Aren't Just for Clothes

Among your siblings or friends, are you the "pretty one," "shy guy," "jock," "smarty," or "artist"? The chances are good you wear at least one *social label* like this depending on the group and situation. But where did this stable of labels come from? The answer might not be as obvious as you may think. Playing sports doesn't mean you're automatically the "the jock" and being quiet in groups isn't always grounds for the "shy guy" label. In fact, activities and behaviors can actually be the *result* of the labels you wear and how you perceive yourself. What do we mean by this? Well, you could go out for sports because you think of yourself as a jock. Or your acceptance of the "shy guy" label might hold you back from speaking up in class or meetings, not the other way around.

The labels we "wear" on the inside combine to create a *self-concept*, or how we see ourselves in relation to others and the world around us. And although you can't imagine not wearing these labels, you didn't start out with them. Your self-concept was made, not born. As a newborn, you didn't have a notion of self. It's not until about six months that we start noticing "self" as distinct from our surroundings. Throughout our childhood, our sense of self is shaped by environmental factors, mainly other people.[1]

Researchers tell us that as we grow up, our self-concept is molded in two primary ways: *reflected appraisal* and *social comparison*.[2] First, we learn and believe who we are and what we're good at when people we trust give us positive or negative feedback. This is reflected appraisal. As a kid, your parents might have told you that you have an ear for music, which led you to pursue voice lessons or take up a musical instrument. Today, your self-concept might include having a "musical gift." On the other hand, you might hold a more negative or neutral idea about yourself based on how parents or other authority figures interacted with you. Perhaps someone in authority declared you "clumsy" or "uncoordinated." This label stuck and ultimately kept you from playing sports. To this day, you think of yourself as "athletically challenged." Or perhaps your sister was always considered the "artistic" one, so you avoided anything to do with art.

We had a student named Mandy, an extremely bright engineering major. Mandy was talkative and consistently had insightful comments during class, so a remark she made during one of her impromptu speeches surprised us. On this particular day, each student was asked to speak on a particular proverb, explain what it meant, and give an example of how it was true or untrue in his or her own life. As expected, Mandy appeared confident in front of the room and spoke well. However, her example threw us. Mandy said the proverb reminded her of her mom, and that she was like her mom in that they were both "airheads." As an aside, Mandy laughingly said that this is what her stepfather routinely called her and her mom.

In our opinion, Mandy was no airhead. Sure, she could sometimes be a little silly and playful, but an airhead? No way. We do know of studies that show that smart girls sometimes "dumb down" so boys don't perceive them as threatening, but that didn't seem to be the case here. Her boyfriend was equally bright and seemed entirely comfortable having a smart girlfriend. In fact, he said he'd won the lottery with brains and beauty. So what stood out in Mandy's case is that she had received this feedback (she's an "airhead") from a seemingly trusted, influential source (her stepfather) and it influenced the way she saw herself.

The second major way our self-concept is developed is by social comparison, which is exactly what it sounds like. In a typical day, we're bombarded by more than 5,000 messages in the form of commercials, Web banners, road signs, and even ring tones. It's almost impossible to resist comparing ourselves to rock stars, fashion models, professional athletes, and really anyone who figures prominently in our cultural landscape. Closer to home, we rank ourselves against our friends, colleagues, coworkers, and even siblings. As adults, this is usually a harmless and fleeting exercise, but during our childhood, this peer comparison made a permanent impression. If we were consistently picked last for a team sport in gym class, our self-concept took notice. When we won first prize in a school spelling bee, it spelled out our future self-concept as well.

Whether formed through reflected appraisal or social comparison, your self-concept is pretty much locked in by the time you turn 30 years old, and can hold a powerful influence over you even when met with contradictory information or when it's proven wrong. But we often don't encounter contradictions later in life, because we gravitate toward people who confirm it for us.

So what does this have to do with public speaking? We carry our self-concept everywhere, especially to the front of an audience. We all have both positive and negative labels that make up our self-concept, but when preparing to give a speech, the negative ones tend to push their way to the front. Our "loser labels" soon overshadow the positive labels and the confidence that goes with it. And even some of the neutral labels we carry can suddenly feel like a liability. For instance, "shy guy" can be fine in some scenarios, but feel like a future fail in public speaking.

Take a few minutes and write down a list of 10 labels, five positive and five negative, that make up your self-concept. These can be anything from physical traits to emotional states, or core values or roles (mom, engineer, daughter, caregiver, son, teacher, brother). Be honest. You're the only person who will see this list. Next, think about how each of these labels might play a role in your public speaking.

If you're like most people, you'll focus pretty heavily on the negative list. That's okay. Spend some time looking it over and deciding how these loser labels are going to hold you back as a public speaker. Then consider how you attained these labels. Who advised you that you shouldn't, couldn't, or wouldn't? What authority figure or social comparison gave you this limiting label? Next, answer these two questions: Do these labels feel shameful? Have these loser labels ever held you back from something you truly wanted or needed to do? If you're like us, our loser labels have been a total drag. It's dragged us away from things we wanted to do, people we wanted to meet, and opportunities that could have improved our life. Chances are good you've had the same experience. At this point, notice how you are feeling. You might feel angry, depressed, sad, confused, or even embarrassed. Whatever you're feeling is fine.

Now, just for kicks, consider that the loser labels you wear might never have really fit from the start, or you've outgrown them. Were you overweight as a kid? Do you still feel like that "fat" kid inside, no matter how much you work out? Maybe you were bullied for being gay in school. Do you still hold onto lingering resentment and shame? Perhaps you were the smallest kid in your crowd and as an adult you still carry that "short guy" attitude around with you. Whatever your story, and believe us, we all have them, it's time to trim the fat, fight back, and stand tall. Because all loser labels are just that, losers, and they are useless to you in public speaking. So, here's what we're going to do: Draw a line (or 10) through each one of these loser labels. Most people focus solely on the loser labels, but you're not going to. You've crossed them out, and that's how they are going to stay. In doing so, hopefully you will begin to realize that loser labels are never productive, helpful, and very often untrue. They have no place in your life and certainly not as a public speaker.

Moving forward! Turn to your list of positive labels. These are your public speaking "superpowers" and the only labels that truly matter in public speaking. Consider how you acquired each of them. What influential person or persons in your life gave you your first taste of confidence, encouraged your talents, or recognized something special in you? How did social comparison influence your super power labels? All of this reflection and nostalgia should feel good, and that's the point.

So hold onto these five superpowers and remember them. You need to refer to them every time you start doubting yourself. And why wouldn't you? Imagine if Spider-Man didn't use his ability to spin webs or Wonder Woman never used her Lasso of Truth, right? It doesn't make any sense. The same goes for you. You've got certified strengths; we all do. Now you need to put them to work. We're not done yet; next, we're going to put a hat on them.

The Hat Trick

Have you ever had to make a good impression? Think about going on a first date or job interview. How did you approach the situation? Were you extra nice or helpful? Did you dress in a certain way? How did you talk? Although we're not always trying to make a good impression, every day we manage our public persona or what some experts call the *presenting self* based on what the situation may call for.[3] At work, you might feel grumpy, but you still smile and greet customers even if you have to fake it. Likewise, our presenting self will adapt to whomever we're interacting with. Do you use the same vocabulary, volume, and speaking rate with a grandparent as you do with your buddies? It's highly unlikely. Your grandparents and buddies see you in different ways. They each expect a different "you," and you give them what they are expecting. Though it sounds calculating to constantly be changing our presenting self to adapt to different situations and people, it's actually necessary and natural. Think of it as always wearing the right hat perfectly suited for every occasion. If people didn't, it would look kind of strange. A motorcycle cop wearing a chef's hat would look odd, not to mention unsafe, and a nun wearing a hard hat at church could send the wrong message.

The truth is, you wear hundreds of hats throughout your life, and you can switch them effortlessly. Picture yourself talking to your sister on the phone when you get a call from your boss. You ask your sister to hold and take your boss's call. As soon as it clicks over to your boss, does your voice change? What about your language and professionalism? You replace your sibling hat with your employee hat in a millisecond. If you didn't, and you spoke to your boss like you do to your sister, he would think you weren't yourself, and in a very real way, you wouldn't be. In the same respect, as soon as you click back to your sister, your sibling hat flips back on and you are instantly casual. See, you don't even think about it; it comes naturally.

When it comes to public speaking, you can use this "hat trick" to your advantage. In other words, when you're public speaking, wear a hat that projects your best, most engaging, and positive self. Just like when looking at our self-concept labels, there might be a tendency to choose an ugly, boring, lackluster, observer, or esteem-sucking hat. These could be "presenting self" hats you might wear as an intern, just-dumped girlfriend, new guy, gopher, credit risk, little brother, or student. Now, put those hats away and pull out the hat you wear when you feel most confident. Which presenting self is most "in charge" and respected? Your hat could be "Sunday School teacher," "artist," or "quarterback." This is the hat—the presenting self—you need to wear as a public speaker. Just like you switch hats for different situations and interpersonal interactions, you can choose which hat to wear when public speaking. So instead of wearing your "just-dumped girlfriend" hat when giving your speech, put on your "Sunday School teacher" hat and use this presenting self or public persona.

If you think this sounds a little crazy, you've got to hear about our Rob. Rob is a successful event planner. His clients include Fortune 500 corporations that hire him to plan big parties for hundreds and sometimes thousands of people. We call him the Traffic Cop because you can usually find him in the center of the action, directing dozens of different people to do a million things. In this element, he's outgoing, can talk to anyone, and can handle any situation that arises without missing a beat. Now, if we were to tell you that Rob is painfully shy, you probably won't believe us. But it's true. In his personal life, he has social anxiety. Attending a concert with friends or going to any size party can be nightmarish for him. In groups, he's never the center of attention and, in fact, doesn't say much. It's hard to imagine this is the same person who is sought after as one of the best event planners in the industry. Yet, it's absolutely the case. He explains it this way: "When I have a job to do, I don't think about being shy. My role as an organizer gives me a purpose for being there. Without it, I am lost and uncomfortable." What does this tell us? It means that it's possible to switch hats when we need to, even against our nature, and in doing so, we can take on the attributes of that particular hat.

Rob's "Traffic Cop" hat gives him the ability to do all kinds of things that he normally wouldn't be able to do in his private life.

We've seen him give an amazing, motivational pep talk to 100 servers and bartenders before a VIP dinner. He's learned that wearing his Traffic Cop hat effectively rids him of insecurities and social anxiety. And it can work for you, too.

Write down which "hats" give you the most confidence during the course of a week. For instance, when you're wearing your "Mom Hat" you know your family depends on you to be the "rock." You are adviser, head cheerleader, shoulder, treasurer, commander-in-chief, culinary whiz, mender of hurt feelings, and mediator. You're also a billion more things. Above all, however, you're not to be messed with when it comes to raising and protecting your kids.

Little League coach is a familiar hat for many dads. Your kids look up to you and count on you in good times and bad. And you'd never let them down. You're a role model and you never forget it. You know that your actions speak louder than words, and you know your words count, too. So when you put on your Little League coach hat, it means something.

Of all the many hats you wear, decide which one gives you the most confidence. Maybe there are two or three. As a public speaker, it's time to put them on.

However, a "presenting self" hat won't cover and shouldn't hide your most obvious physical qualities or other character traits that you can't change. That's why we encourage you to address these head on.

Excuse Me, Your Hair Is on Fire

If your hair were on fire, would you want someone to tell you? Well, duh. Not only would you *want* someone to tell you, you would expect it. But what if your hair was on fire *and* you were about to give a big speech? Again, the answer is obvious. Your message would be meaningless because the flames would make it impossible for you or your audience to concentrate, to say the least. To paraphrase an old American standard, when your hair's on fire, smoke gets in their eyes. We bring up this rather ridiculous scenario to say this: If you have a physical characteristic (for example, height, weight, hair color, manner of speaking, ability of movement) or personality trait you believe makes you a stand out, or be a potential distraction for your audience, it probably will. It might also make you overly self-conscious, inhibiting your ability to effectively share your message. What's the solution? It's almost always better to acknowledge it up-front and with humor if possible. This sounds counter intuitive. Why on earth would a speaker highlight something they felt would be a barrier to reaching his or her audience? The answer is simple: if your audience is focused on the fire, you need to put it out from the beginning.

We once coached a young man originally from India whose first language was Hindi. Arjun was proficient in English, yet he was very concerned that his "accent" would divert his audience's attention from his message. Instead of advising him to practice hiding his nonstandard American accent, we told Arjun to call attention to it. Not only that, we wanted him to do it immediately after he greeted everyone.

On the day of his speech, Arjun got up, smiled, introduced himself and then said to the group of Alabama businesspeople, "Obviously, you can tell from my accent that I was born and raised right here in Birmingham." After half a beat, the audience got the joke and started laughing and clapping. Arjun had engaged his audience by acknowledging what they were all thinking: "Oh, this guy isn't from around here." However, by addressing it himself, and in a joke, he had them tuned in and prepared to hear his message. In this case, what Arjun perceived as a negative worked to break the ice and engage his audience. His accent became an asset. Later, he would tell them a story about how his accent got him tangled up in an awkward and ultimately funny situation, an anecdote to which his audience, with their distinct Southern dialect, could relate. Despite having different ways of articulating things, on this point at least, both Arjun and his audience understood each other perfectly.

Flirt With the Audience...
Not in a Creepy Way

You want to be liked more than you care to admit. Hey, we all do. And being likeable as a public speaker is paramount to an audience accepting your message. So, how do you get people to like you? Well, a lot of us flirt. It's not just a romantic game we play, it's sometimes because we're bored, want something from someone else, or simply because it's fun. As a public speaker, try putting your flirt to work. The same charm you use to disarm a love interest or that crabby "meter maid" to avoid getting a ticket can be used when giving a speech.

You already know the drill. The first order of business is to create interest. How do you create interest? By giving a little and then taking away. This "tease" technique will increase curiosity, which will keep your audience interested. Chip and Dan Heath, authors of *Made to Stick*, suggest that to keep an audience curious, you cannot give away the information like you would be reciting a Wikipedia entry. Rather, create questions that your audience will want to hear the answers to; that is the "tease" part.[4] In other words, they say create a demand for the information before you supply it.

Let's test their theory out. Which of the following two speech "openers" engage you the best?

Global warming kills polar bears.

Imagine a world without polar bears. It's not as farfetched as it sounds. In fact, within your lifetime, most will be extinct. So why are they disappearing?

The first opener is short and not very sweet. It also gives away the ending immediately. It's like a comedienne giving away the punch line in the set up or the world's shortest fairytale: "Once upon a time, they lived happily ever after." However, the second opener creates a scene ("a world without"), then personally invests us in a dramatic outcome ("within your lifetime"), and finally asks a question ("why are they disappearing?"). Translating this into flirting language, you've made eye contact, engaged with a smile, and teased the next topic. Then keep your audience engaged by maintaining good eye contact, using your arms and hands in gestures that invite them in, and walk around so everyone feels a part of the talk, not just the ones in the front row.

Do It With Passion, Or Not at All

What do you care about? Think about it. What riles you, gets your blood boiling, or motivated? It can be as simple as bad drivers or racism. Whatever it is, when you talk about it with your friends or colleagues, you probably do it with a certain amount of passion. This energy comes naturally because you're fired up, but you also want them to feel the same or at least understand why you care so much about this topic, so you let them know how you feel about it through your gestures, eye contact, volume, and vocal variety. In public speaking, the level of a speaker's passion means the difference between the audience caring deeply or tuning out. The truth is, no matter how interesting your subject may be, if you don't show passion for it, you won't get it from the audience. After all, how can you expect them to be interested if you can't muster up a little enthusiasm? We've seen speakers take totally dry and ho-hum topics and charge up the audience's interest because the speaker brought so much energy and life to the topic.

This is especially important when a speaker is talking about highly technical information or the audience is unfamiliar with the topic. Passion also looks a lot like confidence because it gets us out of our head and allows us to speak from the heart. And if you really think about it, when it comes to attraction, there is nothing more appealing (and sexy) than confidence. Passion also shows a commitment to something, and we value that in other people. Many of us lack both confidence and real commitment, and that's why seeing it in others is so magnetic.

One of our clients visited Italy recently. On her return, she was at a coffee shop with a friend sharing stories from her trip, when a complete stranger approached the table and said, "I don't know what you were saying, but you were talking with such passion that whatever it was must have been amazing" and walked away. This is the power of passion. Listening to someone who is passionate about their subject is mesmerizing, even if you're not particularly interested in the topic. It is the person's passion that you are moved by and that captures your attention. According to neuroscientists, this is due to what are called mirror neurons in our brain.[5] These specific type of neurons cause us to feel what someone else is feeling even if we aren't personally experiencing it.

Have you ever gotten teary eyed in a movie when you watched the character cry at losing a loved one? We can "feel" the character's loss. In the same vein, why do you think scary movies are so popular? If they didn't scare us, we wouldn't go to them. The reason we scream, hide our eyes, or leave the theater is because our brain is experiencing what's happening on the screen. If you've seen Stanley Kubrick's classic film *The Shining* (1980) based on the book of the same name by horror master Stephen King, you will never forget the bathroom scene. In the scene, a possessed Jack Torrance, played to perfection by Jack Nicholson, uses an axe to hack his way through the bathroom door to reach his terrified wife, Wendy (Shelley Duvall).

Yep, those are your **mirror neurons** at work. Hopefully, your passion doesn't involve breaking a door down during your speech, or include your audience screaming in sheer terror. However, keep in mind that the focused energy you bring to your delivery can ignite the mirror neurons in your audience, and cause them to feel excited and interested in your topic.

That's why it's critical that you care about your topic, or if you're assigned a topic, you work hard to find something that interests you about it. Dig until you do, because there is nothing more close to death than a dull, dreary, and deflated speaker. Of course, some topics lend themselves to more passion than others, but it's always the speaker's job to bring it. In Hollywood, the joke is that Oscar-winning actress Meryl Streep could read the phone book out loud and make it riveting. It's funny because it's true. Her abilities would allow her to find something creative, intellectually stimulating, or just plain funny about the phonebook. The lesson is this: We give speeches to deliver information, but it should always be done with flare, purpose, and passion. It's your level of passion that will leave your unique thumbprint on the hearts of others. There is always a way.

Scene Stealing

In order to be the Meryl Streep of public speaking, let go of your loser labels and push your positive ones front and center. It's time to shed those old labels that don't define you anymore. You are an adult now and get to decide who you are today. Why in the world would you label yourself with anything other than attributes that support your assets? Along with these positive labels, don't be shy about wearing your most confident hat when it comes to public speaking. This confidence will help you in numerous ways. First, it will allow you to go from hiding to highlighting your most apparent physical characteristics or personality traits, using them to your fullest advantage. Second, let's face it: There is nothing more appealing, and sexy, than confidence. Use it to charm and disarm your audience. And finally, don't forget to bring the passion because the more excited you are about your subject, the more engaged your audience will become. We've all experienced how stimulating it is to notice someone actively listening to what we have to say. All of a sudden anxiety is gone and we are alive in the moment.

Try and Apply

Know Your Labels

Write down your five loser labels and cross them out. Now write down your five winner labels and highlight them. Refer back to your winner labels right before you practice your speech; this will help you speak from that winner place.

Find Your Bad-Ass Hat

Make a list of all of the hats you wear in a week. Which one makes you feel the most confident, the most bad ass? Imagine putting that hat on before you practice your speech and notice how you feel.

Flirting 101

Come up with three questions that will tease your audience into wanting to hear more about your topic. Once you've figured out how to state your topic in a way that captures their attention, insert one of the three questions next; this will their pique their interest and keep them listening.

What Are Your Passions?

Write down the top five things you are passionate about. Don't know? Ask yourself: What pisses you off? What gets your blood boiling? If you had a million dollars to donate, what cause would you donate it to? Who or what would you give your life for? These questions will help you discover your passions. If you have been assigned a topic, find at least two reasons to really care. Design your speech with this in mind.

Key Notes

1. Recognize your label to ensure it isn't working against your public speaking goals. If it is, remember that you weren't born with it and you can change it.

2. Find your most confident hat and put it on every time you practice your speech.

3. If anything may distract from your speech, bring it up at the beginning to turn it into a nonissue.

4. Flirting is not just for love affairs: Engage your audience by teasing your topic and personally investing them in the story.

5. Find at least one thing you can be passionate about in your speech and use that passion to engage your audience.

Chapter 6
Talk Like a Human; Act Like One, Too

Nothing that is complete breathes.

—Antonio Porchia

Chapter Focus
Why seeking perfection is both biological and boring.
Why English majors make bad speechwriters.

Let Your Body Talk

We beg you not to give a perfect speech, especially if your idea of a perfect speech is to deliver every word as practiced, have every gesture timed out, expect laughter or solemn faces in certain places, or otherwise act like a robot. We're not remotely interested in perfect speeches. In fact, the goal is never, ever to give a perfect speech; rather, it's to deliver an authentic one. Robotic speeches are boring, passionless, and mired in contrivance. Perfect speeches require you to focus on precision, as opposed to flexibility. Without flexibility, there is no room for audience engagement, or even, dare we say, accidents. Yes, accidents. They can be beautiful moments of discovery. Visual artists will tell you this. It's the sacred space where an artist can explore and experiment. A drip of unintended color can ignite the senses and cause one to think beyond the original plan. The late British painter Francis Bacon once said, "All painting is an accident." He could "foresee" the image in his mind, but "it transforms itself by the actual paint." Bacon knew the technique of painting. He understood composition and design. But it was the emotional quality of his work that arguably made him one of the greatest and most electrifying artists of the 20th century.[1] To achieve true greatness he had to trust his artistic process and, specifically, the accidents. Celebrated artists like Bacon don't paint by numbers and great speakers shouldn't either.

Just like Bacon, you need to understand the nuts and bolts of public speaking (writing, delivery, how to practice) as well as have a vision of what it will eventually look like, but you also need to allow the process to shape the result. You can't cling so tightly to a specific vision that it smothers creativity. Trusting the process and remaining open to happy accidents will breathe life into a presentation and generate the emotional quality that makes good speeches great. The idea that "anything can happen" also naturally keeps your audience in suspense.

What we are talking about here is called *flow*. In positive psychology it is also referred to as *the zone*. This concept was named by Mihaly Csikszentmihalyi to describe a mental state in which a person is fully immersed in an activity, completely energized by it, and not aware of anything else, including one's own emotions.[2] He believes that everyone can achieve this state of flow while performing most activities that are internally motivated—in other words, that are your choice. Csikszentmihalyi also believes that there are two other components needed to reach the flow state. The challenge level has be high, so taking a bath, although relaxing, will not put you in this flow state. And you need to perceive yourself as very skilled in the activity. By the time you've finished reading this book, you will have all of the criteria met! Because you are reading this, we assume you are internally motivated to become a public speaker. But for those who are forced to learn to public speak due to work or other external reasons (for example, school, work, eulogy, best man's toasts, etc.), there is still some internal motivation at play; otherwise you would have quit your job or simply accepted the consequences that not learning this skill would bring. We have met people who have done both! Also, as you are new to public speaking, the challenge level is high. Finally, by the time you finish the book and have practiced all of the exercises we describe, you will be highly skilled.

A wonderful example of this state of flow is live theater. Many theater actors describe being in a flow state while performing. There is nothing quite like an "as it happens" performance. The energy of the crowd makes it exciting, but it's also knowing that everything is in real time, which means there's no chance for "perfection." No matter how many times the actors have played the role, no two performances are alike. And no two can be completely replicated, which means the audience gets to experience something in that place and time that is wholly unique. At any moment, an actor could discover something new about his character and we can see the revelation manifest before our eyes. Or, a prop can fail and the actors will need to improvise. These kinds of elements bring tension to a live performance. When you watch a great movie, of course there's tension too. Yet these performances are edited. If done well, the pacing is carefully choreographed and the choice of what kind of performance you see is made for you. Filmmaking is a wonderful art form; however, if you're look-ing for the "accident" element, it just isn't there. In public speaking, just like live theater, the accident element is always an undercurrent, keeping things a bit unpredictable.

Now remember we're talking about the "artistic" happy kinds of accidents, not physical ones; and we're not hoping your visual aids will fail. But you should be willing to accept artistic accidents as they come. You might have a light bulb moment about an issue while you're speaking or you may find the powerful, passion-filled voice you never knew you had. These are exciting, magical discoveries and bring an authentic quality you can't get if you've timed every word, gesture, and blink to the second.

Of course, we understand, as a new speaker, there still might be a fear factor about accidents—even happy ones—and you see them as "messing up." Most likely, it's because you're fixating on the accident itself and not on what comes next. And what comes next is what re-ally matters.

Go Ahead, Have a Brain Fart

A student once confessed that one of the things he feared most about public speaking is losing his place mid-sentence. He visualized having what we referred to as a "White Out" in a prior chapter, but is commonly referred to in college vernacular (and some scientific cir-cles) as a "brain fart." So by a show of hands, we asked if his class-mates also dreaded this scenario. The entire class held up their hands. We explained that we would *never* take points off for a brain fart so they shouldn't worry about it.

Quite frankly, we're simply not concerned when people lose their place. *Why should it matter?* What interests us as educators is what happens *after* the brain fart. We're far more interested with how a speaker gets back on track. That's where we see what they're made of. Our only rule is that they don't walk out of the room. And no-body has. In the rare cases when students have had brain farts, they remember our advice to stop talking, not apologize, and think about the last thing they remember saying. Then, based on what they recall saying last, they ask a rhetorical or real question. Within seconds, they are back on track.

Our experience also tells us that if someone does have a brain fart it's pretty well erased from the audience's memory after the speech. We're not kidding. It's because everyone's focus is on what happens after the stumble. Our society loves the underdog and especially when he or she overcomes adversity. That's why you don't focus on falling; you put your energy into getting up.

Write Your Speech to Be Said, Not to Be Read

English majors tend to have the toughest time (at first) in our speech classes. This might seem strange to you. What about the left-brained math and science students? Nope, they do just fine. Although English majors understand the basic outline and certainly the research, it's actually the *writing* that's the problem. This seems crazy. Can't English majors write? Of course, but they're taught to use complex sentence structure and fancy vocabulary. This works out beautifully in essays. Readers have time to absorb and interpret the text. We can go back and reread sections, can look up words we don't know, and are focused just on the task of reading. After all, flipping through *Anna Karenina* and speeding down the freeway would be a tough combination. However, you can't write a speech like you would an essay.

Public speech is meant to be "heard" and must be written in a different style. That's why radio and TV news is written to be *said*, not to be *read*. Broadcasters assume that if you're watching TV news, listening online, or on the car radio, you're also occupied in other ways. For example, we'll have the morning news on when we're getting the kids ready for school, making breakfast, or exercising. Or, we'll have it on in the car while we navigate our way to work. Not only is our attention divided, we only have one chance to hear the information, so journalists share only the most relevant facts and details. In the next few days, spend some time really listening to the news. Though you probably didn't pay much attention in the past, you'll soon notice the difference between broadcast-style writing and what you read in print and online. One of the ways print or online writing differs from broadcast writing is that writers aren't as dependent on "time" to tell their stories, so you'll often find more information than you would in a TV or radio news break. Broadcast writers, on the other hand, will convey only "one thought" per sentence to get their point across. There's rarely a time when you need more than one comma. These short sentences accomplish two things. First, they allow the person reading it out loud to do so with ease. Wordy sentences take longer and are trickier to say. Second, these bite-sized statements also allow the listener to digest information faster, as opposed to chewing on a batch of details all at once.

Public speaking and broadcast style writing use a lot of the same rules. Why? Because if you've ever heard someone read an essay out loud, you know how painful it can be. It's impossible to make essay writing sound conversational. Never-ending sentences collide with mouthfuls of big, unmanageable words. If there is any emotion, the tenor is often academic and it all just comes out limp and lifeless. We're not saying it's bad writing; to the contrary. It just doesn't work for public speaking because it was never intended to be presented out loud. That's why writing to be said, not to be read is the key to a conversational, dynamic, and compelling public speech. If you're new to public speaking, this style might not come naturally for you. After all, it's a different writing approach than most of us have used for years. Fortunately, our method of preparing a speech easily accommodates for this way of writing.

Write Out Loud

The conventional approach to public speaking is to write the speech first, then practice it. Using this method, most new speakers will end up writing an essay, and by the time he or she gets to the practice stage, they're stuck with a "read" not "said" speech. At this point, their only real choice is to go back and do rewrites. They end up spending valuable "practice" time writing, which is double the work. So, if you're at all new to public speaking, or want to really improve your ability to connect with an audience conversationally, you'll want to write and practice *at the same time*. We call it *writing out loud*.

With this approach, you should first write a general outline, jotting down notes or even complete sentences that come to mind. Bullet points work, too. Then, go back to the top and experiment "out loud" how you want to get your points across, working out sentence structure. As you continue to write and rewrite, you should pay careful attention to what it sounds like out loud. Does it come across the way you want it to? Are any word-speed bumps that slow you down or break the flow? How can it be more conversational? What's missing? Trust the process and don't worry about perfection.

Many new speakers will make whatever they write try to sound "smart." Hey, there's nothing wrong with that, unless it stands between you and your audience. Instead of trying to sound smart, work to communicate your ideas. Sometimes we have students who get caught up in "how" to say something. They have the basic idea, but just can't put the sentence together. Everything is jumbled in their head. The concept is there, but the words aren't coming. It happens to all of us.

At this point, we ask them to tell us "what" they're trying to say. Usually, they give us a clear, basic sentence. For instance, "Well, I want to tell the audience we should stop using bottled water because it's harming the environment." Or, "I want them to understand that if you exercise for just 15 minutes a day, you can really improve their health." And 99 percent of the time, that's the perfect sentence to use in the speech. Fancy sentences are fine, but it's the message that counts the most.

As you continue to write and read out loud, your speech will start to take shape. A key thing to remember, however, is that this process takes time. And it should. Work on it, walk away, come back to it, and read it out loud again. With time, you'll be shocked at how good it will start to sound and how confident you will start to feel about your upcoming speech.

As mentioned, writing out loud breaks conventional wisdom, but you're guaranteed to end up with a speech to be said, not read. And although that was the original reason to write your speech this way, there are other major bonuses. First, we've found that when most people go the traditional route and write their speech first and practice it second, they'll dedicate at least 98 percent of the time to the writing and leave just the remaining fraction to practicing. This inevitably leads to a very rocky delivery, and can be very disheartening for the speaker who might then erroneously believe that they are just a terrible public speaker. In reality, it just means they didn't practice nearly enough. The truth is that you can't over-practice. It's impossible. And hear us when we tell you that when you sit down after your speech, no matter how much you practiced, you'll wish you practiced more. Our method of writing out loud solves this issue organically because you're practicing and subconsciously memorizing as you're writing. So, by the time you're finished writing, you'll probably have most of your speech memorized—or at least the key points. Additionally, you will have also worked out the best way to deliver certain words and phrases for maximum effect. You'll have the cadence, inflection, and volume down. It's the most effortless and pressure-free way to memorize. Then you can spend your practice time, practicing.

The second major benefit is that you'll know exactly what you're saying. In other words, you will be forced to examine each word and phrase carefully, because you've had to say it out loud, not just heard it in your head. In our head, it's easy to skim words we don't know or ignore whole passages. Have you ever read a book, started daydreaming, and after 20 minutes you realize you've read an entire chapter, but can't remember what it was about? You've turned the pages and everything! Personally, and we're not proud of this, we've read entire books (usually fantasy or sci-fi) not knowing how to pronounce the names of the main characters. We can get away with this when we say it in our head, but if we were ever asked to use the character names out loud, we'd be busted.

If you write your speech first, and only practice when you're done, you'll have extra work to do and it will cut into your practice time. That's because when we do it this way, our brain goes on autopilot when it comes to the smallest details, skipping words or phrases we can't pronounce because we don't have to in that moment. Writing out loud forces us to figure out how to pronounce unfamiliar words and names. It also connects us to the words in our speech in a more direct manner than just reading it in our head. This matters because knowing how to pronounce words and understand key phrases will save you a lot of embarrassment. Nothing kills credibility faster than a speaker, who is supposed to be an expert, mispronouncing proper names and technical or medical terminology. Writing out loud cures this fast.

It's News to Me

Do you remember the last time you went through a drive-through window at a fast food restaurant? You have to give your order to a box. The information is transmitted to a person in the restaurant who enters the order into the system. It rarely goes smoothly. It's often like the game "telephone" we played as kids, where a clear message is ultimately undecipherable to the person on the receiving end. Somehow it works out because, even though you sort of understand what they're saying, they hear *you*. It gets more complicated when it's critical for you to understand *them*.

Most fast food restaurants ask employees to do "suggestive selling."[3] It's usually a way to promote a new menu item and increase sales. Let's say that that's exactly the case with a fictional restaurant chain called Burger Blaster. Corporate has asked that drive-through employees at every restaurant suggest the company's newest burger before taking a customer's order. On the day of the big rollout, an order taker comes on shift. Her manager tells her, "We're promoting a new burger. It's called 'Honey-Glazed Miracle on a Bun.' Please suggest that to every customer when taking an order." That's simple enough. She's just learning about this new burger and wants to get it right. She writes it down so she can refer to it. The order taker is ready to suggest it when the first car comes through. She says carefully, "Welcome to Burger Blaster, would you like to try our new 'Honey-Glazed Miracle on a Bun' today?" The customer considers it and says, "Sure, why not?" Mission accomplished. The next car also agrees to this new delicious-sounding sandwich. About 20 minutes into her shift, however, orders stop coming in for the "Honey-Glazed Miracle on a Bun." In fact, for the rest of her shift, she doesn't get a single order. Is it because word got out that the burger was awful? Maybe, but the more accurate reason might be that once the order taker got familiar with saying "Honey-Glazed Miracle on a Bun," she began to say it faster and faster, and without any special emphasis. So, what customers heard when they pulled up was: "WcomeBurlaster, wooluulikemircallbuoay?" Our order taker doesn't realize that just because she knows what she's saying, it is completely new information to the customers. And because of her garbled, rushed delivery, customers have no idea what she said.

Most people who come to Burger Blaster have made up their minds by the time they get to the order box, so to figure out what the heck the box just said feels like too much trouble. This scenario happens at all 1,400 Burger Blaster locations. What's the result? The "Honey-Glazed Miracle on a Bun" promo item looks like a bust for Burger Blaster and, so, Corporate takes it off the menu. This is all hypothetical and perhaps a bit extreme, but can you see this happening? Of course, because it's happened to you. How many times has the box spewed out some words that sound like it could be a new menu item, but sounded suspiciously like a "Mayonnaise Pasted Karp Mobile?" Yum. We'll take five.

This brings us back to your speech. As you're writing your speech out loud, you'll become familiar with new phrases and terminology, which will make you more confident. But be careful that this familiarity doesn't derail your delivery. Because when we know words well, we have a tendency to say them very quickly or not give them much emphasis. After all, you know how to pronounce them correctly and understand what they mean, but your audience might not. They haven't spent hours preparing and practicing with you. So, be sure you take the time to highlight these words, setting them off by saying them more slowly, and perhaps pausing before and after. If you don't, your audience might miss them. And if hearing them is critical to understanding your message, you could get drowned out and Corporate might cancel your new idea, too.

Boldface and Highlight Words

Along with introducing new words and information to your audience, you also need to boldface and highlight key words that have the ability to supercharge your message. We call these *impact words*. An impact word shows value, acts as a qualifier, or is a proper name. Value words relate to numbers (million, billion, trillion) or statistics (90 percent, two-thirds). Qualifiers are words like "however," "but," "yet," "therefore," and so on. You need to give these words punch. Proper names are names of people or places and should be highlighted so they stand out. This means slowing down and emphasizing the words, as opposed to running through them. Usually, these words lend credibility to your topic. When an audience hears, "according to *Harvard* University researchers" it means something. On the other hand, saying, "accordinglyarvarsity" only means they can't understand what you said.

Anchors and hosts use impact words and highlight them in delivery. So listen for these as well. You probably haven't been paying much attention to them, but it's one of the reasons you are able to grasp a news story so quickly. Broadcast journalists help the listening audience and you should help your audience, too.

Let Us Hear Your Body Talk

Your mouth isn't the only part of your body involved in public speaking. Although it's where the words come out, the rest of your body does a lot of talking. In fact, experts say that up to 93 percent of a message's emotional impact is derived from nonverbal cues.[4] To put it simply, actions often speak louder than words. Whether you realize it or not, in every interaction, you can read or misread these cues in other people, and they are doing the same with you. These interpretations come naturally.

When it comes to public speaking, our body does a lot of talking. And for new speakers this can be disconcerting. This is primarily because public speaking is not exactly something you're used to. Standing up in front of a bunch of people can feel like a giant spotlight is on you and is following your every move. So our body responds in different ways. Some of us just freeze up. Suddenly, we go rigid and our movements (when we do make them) seem stilted and jerky. If we're not frozen, we're fidgety. We've seen speakers pace wildly back and forth. Others are constantly shifting, and still others (especially women) are wrapping their legs into a pretzel. Why? Because you don't know what to do with yourself.

There are two ways to get comfortable with the spotlight on you. First, you have to practice standing up in front of a room with your hands at your sides. This could be any room; your living room works. Even though you won't have an audience in your own living room, the key is to get used to standing still with your hands at your sides. The point is to get used to this stance because it is not natural, so by the time you get up to deliver your speech, it will be a little more familiar. Guys should stand shoulder width apart and women can bring their feet closer to together. Relax your shoulders. Bend your knees just a touch once in a while. If you're differently abled, we still need you up front and center. Try just "being" up there for two minutes, just looking out. We're not going to lie; it's super awkward the first time. But it doesn't *look* awkward. It actually looks just fine, even natural. What screams "unnatural" is being totally rigid or running around the room like someone with ants in their pants. When you're frozen, we interpret this as complete terror. If you're fidgety, we see nervous energy that is not sure where to go. Either way, the message is uncomfortable for the audience and we're totally distracted from anything coming out of your mouth. After a few times, it doesn't feel as weird or silly. If you notice that you start shifting or pacing while standing in your living room, accommodate for it by putting books or something heavy on your feet. If you should freeze up, shake it out.

The second way to get comfortable—or at least look that way—is to move. In this case, we're talking about gestures. Some of us grew up in households where everyone talked with his or her hands. Others were raised in cultures that viewed big or a lot of gestures as rude. Whatever the case, you should strive to have some movement, in the form of gestures, in your speech. Gestures are very helpful in emphasizing a point. Besides, it's far more interesting for the audience and the speaker if there's movement. So, how do you know what gestures to use and when?

Our advice: Don't plan them strategically. If you have three points, don't consciously think, "Gee, I better hold up three fingers." Inevitably, it feels staged and your body will betray the lie. Remember you're a human, not a robot. Fortunately, you don't have to overthink what gestures to use and when to apply them, because your body is an excellent communicator and it already knows. All you have to do is ask it.

The fastest, most direct way to figure out the most appropriate gestures is to do your speech without words. Imagine you're playing a game of charades and you must communicate the content of your speech using only hand signals and your body to tell the story. But make it life or death. You must communicate this message to your audience or someone is going to die. Go wild. Start at the beginning of your speech and go all the way through. Do whatever it takes until you're convinced that the audience will understand your message strictly through your body movement. Maybe you can ask a friend to help you out by playing "the audience." So what's the point of this exercise? Your body is more than capable of communicating your speech without sound. But note that if you're too self-aware and you stop, this exercise won't work. So commit to it. When you do, you'll discover something pretty amazing.

After you've run through your speech using only your body to communicate the message, try your speech again (this time out loud), letting your body do your bidding. Allow it to speak along with you. You need not do anything special. Just start your speech and unconsciously, and without any extra effort, your body will gesture appropriately. Don't worry, they won't be huge, outrageous, charade-like movements. Your body knows better than that. Instead, it will speak along with you with just the right body visuals to reinforce and support the audible portion of your speech. We use this exercise in our classes all of the time. Initially, it never fails that our students look at us like we have completely lost it. After the exercise is over, we have them come up one by one and give their speech in front of the class. When they begin to notice how much looser their body feels and that it actually is "going with the flow" of the speech, they completely get the point of the exercise. And we have, once again, gained our credibility back!

Lose Your Cool

This chapter might have seemed a little whacky to a few of you. It goes against a lot of conventional wisdom about how to prepare to give a speech. We are asking you to see things from a new perspective and trust the process. As you read through this chapter, some of you might have already decided that you won't be caught dead just standing still in front of your living room. Or, you're not about to start acting like a fool by giving your speech without words, even if no one is watching. Okay. That's your choice. But what do you want? If it's to be an amazing public speaker, you have to lose your cool. You have to be willing to be a little nuts, act a bit silly, and take risks. Because as bizarre as a lot of these exercises sound, the results are undeniable. You will be a better speaker, period.

Know this: You don't become more confident *after* you are a successful public speaker; the confidence starts from within, right now. Remember that part about "nothing is more appealing (or sexy) than confidence"? When you really, truly commit to these techniques, you'll carry yourself differently—not just in front of an audience, but through life, knowing that you showed up for yourself, and were willing to step outside of your comfort zone and possibly fall down. So what's it going to be? Are you going to stay small and scared speechless, or are you going to lose your cool and get down to business?

Try and Apply

How Does it Sound?

After you've come up with your outline, start to fill it in "out loud" and record yourself. This is not to hear what you sound like; it is simply so you don't have to worry about stopping your "flow" to write down that brilliant thing that just came out of your mouth.

Recouping After a Brain Fart

As we pointed out, forgetting your speech is not usually the problem, it's how you get back on track that separates the men from the boys or the women from the girls. Come up with a few rhetorical questions (like we suggested in Chapter 1) that are related to your speech in a general way that you can use at any time to pose to the audience. This will buy you time to find your place. We have found that preparing for a brain fart decreases the likelihood of having one!

What Words Are You Going to Boldface and Highlight?

Go through your speech, find your value words, qualifiers, and proper names and highlight them. Practice your speech out loud emphasizing these words. Did you notice a difference?

Practice Your Speech Without Words

Call a friend over and have some fun with it! See if they can guess what you're trying to say. After you have "charaded" your speech to them, practice giving it out loud and ask them how you did. Notice how you felt afterward. Did your body feel a little looser than before the game of charades, a little more "in the flow"?

Key Notes

1. Perfection is not for speeches: Being prepared is important, but being flexible while delivering your speech will win you the gold.

2. If a brain fart happens, the important part is the recovery; and that's what the audience will remember.

3. Write out loud: While you're creating your speech, speak it out loud and write down what *sounds* best to generate a speech to be said, not read.

4. Don't play telephone: Highlight difficult sounding words, practice them, and remember to say them slowly while delivering your speech.

5. Impact words: Emphasizing your impact words will help them stand out.

6. Actions speak louder than words: Do not forget your body while delivering your speech. Practice *saying* it without words.

Chapter 7
The 7 Deadliest Speech Sins

Be sincere; be brief; be seated.

—Franklin Delano Roosevelt

Chapter Focus
Why we fall for fallbacks (old habits, ways of thinking).
How to kill a speech in seven ways and fast fixes.

Why We Fall for Fallbacks

Change is painful; no, really it is. It feels physiologically uncomfortable. It takes more energy and effort to do something new than to do something we are used to doing. If you have ever tried driving in England (or if you're English, driving in the United States), on the other side of the street, you know how stressful and uncomfortable that can feel. When we have done something over and over, it exits the "thinking" part of the brain (the *prefrontal cortex*) and gets stored in a deeper part of the brain (the *basil ganglia*). This function is important because the thinking brain tires easily and can only hold a limited amount of information at any given time. If we wasted time and energy consciously thinking about the things we automatically do, like getting dressed, brushing our teeth, combing our hair, making our breakfast, or driving our car, we'd be exhausted by the time we got to work! The basil ganglia, on the other hand, functions very well without conscious thought expending low energy and little effort for any routine behavior or habit. This leaves us with enough juice to do everything else we're going to accomplish in a day.[1]

Neuroscientists have discovered something else about our brain that gets in the way of change and they call it the *walk toward, run away* theory. Maximizing our rewards (walk toward) and minimizing our threat (run away) is what motivates most of our behavior.[2] Frankly, it would be weird if the opposite were true. Guess we would be able to take on anything and there would be no need for this book, but nonetheless, it would be odd if we were motivated to do things that felt threatening. On top of this motivation to walk toward rewards, our brain has an incredible capacity to detect "errors" between what we expect and what is actually occurring. Anything that is different from what we expect sends a signal to our brain's threat detector and we go into high alert. This state of high alert is stressful, causing us to act more impulsively and become more emotional. Learned behaviors and habits become expectations to our brains, so even changing *maladaptive* **habits** can send a message that something is wrong, triggering our error threat detector.

Many of us have developed bad habits, including maladaptive speech patterns like "um," "like," "I mean," and "you know?" In our daily conversations, we all have our go-to phrases; let's call them *filler words*. But most language we use is out of complete habit, including our filler words, and is often unintentional. We don't even notice we use this type of language. When you hear other people say "um" 20 times in a row (not that you would, unless you were listening for it), they don't realize it either. If they did, they would probably stop. The important thing here is to make sure you're not including them in your speeches. Public speaking is a conversation, but it's the most elevated kind, so your language must reflect this fact. It's critical for you to identify and curb any bad habits or filler words that might disconnect or alienate your audience. Your audience expects you to be an expert and experts aren't supposed to use "um," "like," "I mean," and "you know." One great way to rid your speeches of fillers is to stop using them in your daily conversations. It takes a bit of effort at first, and you may not notice when they're gone, but other people will! This chapter will cover the most common deadly speech sins by helping you become aware of them. Then we'll give you more tools to retrain your tongue.

Deadly Speech Sin #1: Killer Fillers

"T'aint What You Do (It's the Way That You Do It)" wrote jazz musicians Melvin "Sy" Oliver and James "Trummy" Young, a sassy song first recorded in 1939. It's certainly a sound suggestion when giving a speech. In public speaking, "how" you say something is sometimes more important than "what" is said. If you've ever heard a speaker with a bad run of the "ums," you know exactly what we're talking about. She might have important or interesting things to convey, but her way of sharing it (for instance, saying "um" a thousand times) gets in the way. Speech stumbles are sometimes called disfluencies or *segregates*. Most often, these are "fillers"—words that don't contribute much to a sentence other than give us time to think of what to say next. The most commonly used fillers include "you know," "and stuff," "like," "uh," and "um." Fillers are often uttered unconsciously, but too many of them can make us question a speaker's expertise, authority, or, like, um, credibility, you know? There is some debate about *why* we use them, but linguistics professor Mark Liberman says we know there is a definite gender split when it comes to actual usage. He found that men say "uh" 25 percent more than women, whereas women say "um" 22 percent more than men.[3] Which do you use? Even if you're unsure, we've still got a cure, and we'll get to that in a minute. But first, let's highlight one verbal segregate that you're probably unaware you're even using.

Deadly Speech Sin #2: A Mean Case of "I Mean"

Perhaps no verbal segregate is more nonsensical than the filler "I mean." I mean, you hear it everywhere. The phrase "I mean" is meant to correct what you have just said or to add more information. However, far too many otherwise-smart people are using the expression to *start* new sentences. It is a wholly improper way of speaking. We challenge you to listen to interviews, lectures, even conversations, and count the times you hear people begin a fresh sentence with this vile verbal segregate. We really mean it. It might surprise you. Though the practice annoys us to no end, as a public speaker it should be used properly or evicted from your vocabulary. This horrendous habit tells the listener that you, the speaker, are not very aware of what's coming out of your mouth and in the case of public speaking, that's not a good thing.

So, let's say you are a big fan of the "fillers." Maybe you have a mean case of the "I means" or, um, can't stop saying "uh." What do you do? That's easy. Stop doing it. Okay, maybe it's not so simple if you've made fills a part of your speech pattern. Here's the fast fix. First, be aware of how you talk in normal conversation and begin to notice how others are speaking well. Second, when you hear yourself using a filler, stop and correct yourself. In many cases, you can replace the filler with a pause. Listen, you don't need to fill up every second of silence. And in this case, silence can be golden. When you practice your speech, you should also record yourself. Truly this is one of the worst, but most essential experiences of a new public speaker's life. Just know that it's usually accompanied with "Wait, I sound like *that*?!" But, really, as painful as it is at first, if you're going to perfect your pitch and poise, you have to know how you sound. When we get to practice techniques, we'll be sure to remind you again. Lucky you. And remember: Focus is your golden ticket. As you're noticing how you talk, focus on every word. That focus will help you notice when a filler word shows up in your mind and then you can consciously choose not to use it. This very purposeful behavior will get the fillers out of your speech and clean up your delivery.

Deadly Speech Sin #3: Uptalk

Though once lampooned as "Valley Girl" talk, ending declarative sentences in a question is now unnecessarily ubiquitous for most Americans under 30. Technically, it's called a *high-rising terminal*, but also known in the United States as uptalk or upspeak. It's generally agreed to have first surfaced in Los Angeles's San Fernando Valley and spread like a verbal virus via popular music, TV, and films to the rest of the country, who adapted it into their daily delivery.[4]

So what's the problem? First, not everything is a *question*. Second, it makes your speech pattern immensely uninteresting and repetitive. Quite frankly, the lack of any downward inflections at the end of sentences is just lazy. Remember not everything is a question, so don't make everything coming out of your mouth into one. Third, it sends a powerful message to an audience—and in the most negative way. Questions are asked rhetorically, or to elicit a yes or no response. How can you possibly show credibility if you apparently have to get confirmation on everything you say? This speech style might also cost you a job or big promotion. Studies have shown that bosses hate uptalk and often associate it with a lack of confidence and intelligence.[5] If you do get into an executive position and you're an uptalker, your ability to give clear and authoritative direction might be missing. Let's imagine a sales manager is giving her team a sales goal. Using uptalk, she says: "We have to raise our quarterly figures by 25 percent?" Okay, does she want them to raise sales figures or not? She's made a statement into a question and, in so doing, has consciously or unconsciously cost herself credibility with her team.

As a public speaker, your job is to exude confidence. You're not going to accomplish this by asking for permission about everything you say.

Deadly Speech Sin #4: Podiums and Pretzel Legs

We love to stand behind podiums or anything that will serve as a barrier between the maddening crowd and us. Even though we have already established that the audience is not our enemy, somehow we still believe a podium will protect us from some hidden danger (see: primitive brain).

Another reason why we hide behind podiums is because most people have no idea what to do with their legs during a speech. Although many of us think nothing of standing in general, when it comes to giving a public speech, we are suddenly posture-challenged.

So, here are some fast fixes. The best advice for guys is to stand with your legs shoulder width apart and keep your weight evenly balanced while bending your knees just slightly. You don't want to lock your knees because it slows down blood circulation and you'll end up giving your speech on the floor. Women should stand legs apart with 5 to 7 inches between their ankles—whatever is most comfortable. However, we've noticed that a lot of young women won't stay in this position very long. Within minutes they will cross one leg over the other, shifting their body into a pretzel-like position worthy of Cirque du Soleil. You know who you are, ladies. Not knowing how to position yourself properly and plain-old jitters are the main reasons for this cross-legged conundrum, but it sends a nonverbal signal that you lack confidence and any kind of authority. And that's the last thing you want when giving a speech.

If you find yourself in this pretzel-like predicament or your feet have a way of wandering, try putting something heavy on top of them when you're practicing. Yes, we're serious. Use books or a backpack, anything that will force you to keep your dogs on the leash.

Once you've got your sure footing, you can practice walking. Yes, most of us forget how to walk, too. If you want to move left or right during your speech, just make sure you lead with the outside leg first. For example, if you want to go left, lead with your left leg. This side step looks smooth and helps avoid turning too far away from your audience.

Finally, get in the helpful habit of not using a podium unless absolutely necessary. Why? Because unless you plan to carry a podium around with you, you're not always going to have one. When you learn to let go, the lack of a podium will never throw you off track.

Deadly Speech Sin #5: Speed Kills

Thanks to nerves, many of us start talking very quickly when giving speeches. But speed can kill a great speech. If the audience can't keep up with you, they won't. Going over your normal speed limit also opens you up to stumbles, fumbles, and verbal spills. However, most of us can keep up with a fast talker if he starts out slowly enough for us to catch his cadence. It's like riding on the subway. Once you're on board the car, speed is no problem, but there's a reason you don't board when it's going 55 mph. The same goes with public speaking. An audience has no problem keeping up once they're "on board" your speaking rate, but you must give them time to get seated.

So how do you teach yourself to do this? Here's the fast fix. We call it the "hammer trick." If you've ever hammered anything—no, not "gotten" hammered; that's something very different. Where were we? Oh yes, if you've ever hammered a nail, you know that you don't start swinging super fast right away. You carefully determine the distance from the hammer to the nail, and the first couple of swings are usually pretty slow. This is to make sure you drive the nail into its proper place, not into your thumb. Remembering how to use a hammer will remind you to start out slow, allowing the audience to easily get in time with your tempo.

Deadly Speech Sin #6:
"Does That Make Sense?"

Maybe it's just us, but ending any verbal statement with the question "Does that make sense?" just cost you your credibility. If you have to ask, it doesn't and if you're asking as a way to engage the audience, you're not. You're losing them because now they think they are wasting their precious time listening to someone who didn't bother to practice their speech to ensure it made sense. Lastly, if you're trying to assess whether your audience understands what you're saying (while preparing your speech, run it by your friends to *make sure* it makes sense), there are better and more effective ways of figuring out if you're losing your audience. Their body language, eye contact, and occasional head nodding (the subtle, up-and-down "I get it" kind, not the slow, down-moving chin resting against my chest as in "I fell asleep" kind) will certainly clue you in. If that question is part of your regular speak, lose it now!

Deadly Speech Sin #7:
Marble Mouth Mayhem

Are you a mumbler? We call this malady "Marble Mouth" because it sounds suspiciously like you're speaking with a mouth full of marbles. If people are always asking you to repeat yourself, you could be one of these diction-afflicted folks. Maybe you have a family member or chum who has the undesirable distinction of merging words into a mangled mess? Whatever the case, it's time to start "sounding out" and "speaking up." After all, if you mumble through your speech, what's the point? Your audience will surely miss most of your amazing message. Not to fear! It takes just a minute, not a year, for our miraculous, sure-fire cure. And the next time someone asks, "Have you lost your marbles?" you can smile and say, "Yes, and it was a no-brainer."

"Straight From the Horse's Mouth" Warm-Up

Without further ado, here's the marvelous one-minute miracle method guaranteed to make you lose your marbles, and it's "Straight from the Horse's Mouth." Use it daily, or just whenever you're called into public speaking service.

What you will need: a clean pen or pencil, this book, and your complete commitment.

Step One:

Read the first paragraph titled "Marble Mouth Mayhem," straight through, aloud. Do your best to articulate every word.

Step Two:

Immediately after you've finished reading the paragraph, put a clean pen or pencil into your mouth horizontally (like a horse's bit) and push it back between your top and bottom teeth until it's slightly uncomfortable. Your lips should not be able to touch easily. Now, read the paragraph titled "Marble Mouth Mayhem" again, straight through, aloud. Again, do your best to articulate every word. Really work hard to make yourself understandable, and we know this isn't easy with a pen or pencil in your mouth. Don't give up, pause, remove the pen, or otherwise interrupt the flow of your speaking. Yes, you will sound strange. However, this exercise is *only* effective if you commit to it. Otherwise, you won't hear or feel the full benefits.

Step Three:

Right after you finish reading the paragraph a second time, re-move the pen or pencil from your mouth and read the paragraph a final time, straight through, aloud. Do your best to articulate every word.

What did it sound like when you read the paragraph the final time? How did it make you feel? If you've done the steps correctly, the third time should have been a charm! In only one minute, your words went from mush to magic, which very likely gave you a surge of confidence. All it took was 60 seconds, a pen or pencil, and a little motivation.

Salvation Is Within Reach

As you read through the deadly speech sins, don't fret if you are a "sinner" of one or all seven. You are not doomed into a life of flunky, flawed patterns of behavior and horrible habits. Refocusing will set you free and allow you to give the best speech of your life! As we have mentioned before, research has shown that purposeful, focused, and intentional behavior can overcome the brain's resistance to change. However, if you are really serious about rewiring your brain, you're going to have to focus your attention on this new behavior and practice it often. This *hyper* focus on the new behavior is literally creating new connections while the old ones get shut down for business. Let's add another step to this, compliments of neuroscience research[6], and include a motivator that rewards your new behavior. Practice your exciting new behaviors in front of your friends and have them give you positive feedback; bribe them if you have to! Positive feedback feels like a reward to your brain, and you know what they say about humans and rewards: We love them! Focusing on the new behavior and getting a positive reaction from your *bribed* friends will cause your brain to calm the threat detector. With practice, these new behaviors will graduate from your prefrontal cortex to your basil ganglia allowing them to become expected habits. One less thing to think about when captivating your audience!

Try and Apply

Know Your Deadly Sins

We hope you have taken our advice and taped yourself. The only way to find out where you are "sinning" is to hear it for yourself. We have a tendency to rate ourselves better than we really are. Now, rest assured, we are not trying to discourage you, but we want you to be honest with yourself so you can be consciously aware of all of your deadly sins. Awareness is the first step to change.

Focus and Be Purposeful

Once you have become aware of your speech faux pas, practice it again paying very close attention to every word you are saying. Notice when the urge comes up to say or do the speech killer, and stop. In that moment, become aware of what just happened: Were you getting nervous? Did you start thinking about the audience watching you? Did you realize you forgot what came next? Immediately repeat the sentence three times without the speech killer, focusing on every word and then start over. This focused "stop and repeat action" will be remembered by the brain, and chances are that next time this line comes around, you will be able to keep the killers out of the speech.

Key Notes

1. Killer fillers: Become aware of your killer fillers; the more aware you are, the less you will use them.

2. The "I Means": It is a given that you are saying what you mean. Saying "I mean" is just redundant!

3. Uptalk: Make sure you are ending what you say as a question *only* if you are asking a question.

4. Pretzel legs: Keep your legs in mind while you practice your speech to avoid pretzel legs while you deliver your speech.

5. Speed kills: Practice saying your speech slowly, so on speech day you stay within the speech speed limit.

6. "Does that make sense?" should never be asked while delivering a speech, or anywhere, anytime, ever.

7. Marble Mouth: Practice your speech while holding a pencil in your mouth to ensure you will be able to enunciate all the words correctly on speech day.

Chapter 8
Address the Dress

It starts with the shoes.

—Marina Sirtis

Chapter Focus
Why comfort counts when it matters the most.
How to dress the part without falling apart.

Clothing Communicates

If you've ever felt extremely underdressed at an important event, you know the definition of "awkward." Suddenly, you want to crawl underneath the table. You can't wait to get out of that party you were really looking forward to. And, why didn't your girlfriend tell you "no shorts" (she did) or that her parents would be there (she did, twice)? So, you ditch the dress-down disaster as fast as possible, languish in "liquid courage," or spend most of the night hiding behind large planters. No matter how hard you try, however, self-consciousness and a negative internal dialogue paralyze you. Did her mom just roll her eyes at you?

But why does something as simple as breaking a dress code make us crazy? It's because (accurate or not) you are absolutely convinced everyone is staring at you and silently taking notes on your terrible attire. And, although it may only *feel* like they're staring, people will make a judgment based on what you're wearing. You don't have to be terribly observant or even fashion conscious to be an excellent and quick evaluator. We're not talking about a fun (or snarky) fashion critique; it's our primitive defense instincts at work and a snap judgment. It's how we determine whether a stranger is friendly, dangerous, like us, from another culture, rich, poor, gay, straight, laid back, professional, and otherwise. In a split second, we check off a list in our head and determine how to approach or avoid someone unfamiliar to us. It's a defense mechanism honed from years of personal and anecdotal experience with a variety of people. Are we right all the time? Of course not, but it's our brain's way of protecting us. We tend to more likely help people who we perceive as more similar to us.[1] So dressing the part, depending on where you are going, can help in more ways than one.

What? Wait, Your Shirt Is Saying Something...

The fact is that clothes do communicate, even if *we* (the wearer) can't hear them. And it's not just about how well dressed *or not* we are or whether we assess someone as safe to approach. Studies show that assumptions about someone's personality, level of confidence, and socioeconomic status can be part of the overall assessment.[2] In addition, if you want to be seen as an authority in your field, you're better off dressing in a more conservative way. The higher up in status, the more it matters if that top button on your shirt is fastened or unfastened.[3] Now, we can almost hear some of you saying, "I would never judge someone's personality just based on what they're wearing! How dare you suggest such a thing!" Okay, so maybe you don't sound so dramatic. The truth is that judging someone on what they're wearing is automatic and mostly unconscious. We all do it, but for the most part we are not fully aware of our judgments. However, they may show up in the decisions we make. For example: who you trust, whose advice you take, or even if you believed the information received in a lecture.

The clothes you choose to wear not only send a message to the people around you, but they also send a message to *you*, the wearer! We have all noticed the difference between wearing business attire versus workout clothes. And most of us have had the experience of how much better we feel when we dress up after wallowing in sweats, ice cream, and a Bridget Jones marathon after a breakup. Did you know there's a name for that? Just when you thought you had heard it all. It's called *enclothed cognition* and it is defined as "the systematic influence that clothes have on the wearers' psychological process."[4] So this is about what the clothes we wear are communicating to *us*. An important finding from this research that pertains to you, the speech giver, is that putting on certain clothes can prepare you to take on different roles and can also affect your abilities. Actors experience this often and in interviews have said that putting on the character's clothes helped them get into the role. Take a moment to think which clothes help you feel strong, empowered, and confident. The take away here is that you should choose your dress not based on how you feel, but on how you *want* to feel on speech day.

Of course, we're not saying smother your real personality or even refrain from making a "statement" with your clothing, but we want to emphasize that even bold choices have natural boundaries in the form of set or unwritten protocols. For instance, at most funeral services, donning an architecturally daring hat might turn heads, but it's a lot more conventional and acceptable than, say, sporting a banana yellow bikini. As a public speaker, your attire sets the tone for how your audience will accept or "reject" you. Clothing has the effect of distancing you from your audience or bringing you closer together. Of course, the closer the audience feels to you, the more open they will be to hearing your message.

This is why you won't ever catch a male political type wearing a blazer, silk tie, and fancy loafers while downing a cold one with his constituents at a local pub. At the very least, the politicos roll up their sleeves, ditch the coat, and loosen the tie. Likewise, a female politician wouldn't visit voters at a Minnesota turkey farm wearing heels and pearls. On the other hand, when keynoting a political party convention or speaking on the floor of Congress, you won't see these same folks in work boots and hardhats. They dress for their role, event, and audience and you should, too.

So what's an appropriate look? Of course, the first rule is to be you. There is nothing worse than feeling both uncomfortable in your clothes and managing nerves at the same time. However, you need to balance that idea with what is appropriate for your role and who is in your audience. To start, what's your role at the event? In some cases, there is a "uniform" that automatically accompanies your role. If you're taking part in a religious service or academic ceremony (like graduation), wardrobe is usually clearly specified. The same goes for weddings and other events for which attire is mentioned on the invite. But just keep in mind that not all definitions of "business attire" are the same. Weather and location also demand different adjustments. If your role is at an unfamiliar event or occasion, try to find out what people wore the year before or at similar occasions. Photos of the event might be posted on social media, an event Website, or otherwise. Ask around. Find an appropriate look or style, and then upgrade it just a notch. You are, after all, going to be out in front, so you want to look and feel sharp. The overall message you want to send is "I respect this occasion and you, as an audience."

We always encourage students to dress up on speech day. First, it communicates to the professor you have made the extra effort because you are taking the assignment seriously. Second, other students are more apt to give you their attention because your attire communicates professionalism. Third, remember enclothed cognition? We all tend to carry ourselves differently when we're wearing more professional attire.

Ladies, we act differently when we're wearing heels, as opposed to flip-flops. Physically, we have to adjust our posture. You probably stand a little straighter and walk a little more purposefully (if only not to wipe out on a slick floor). Guys, a suit and tie change the game for us as well. And it's not just feeling more "put together" that makes us strut a bit more assuredly, it's also the positive attention we get from others that puts the style in our stride.

A Word About Hats

Unless you have a royal title or are giving a speech in England, hats can distract and hinder. You may not be aware of how you hide underneath your hat, but your audience will. Speaking of hiding your game face: Guys we know you love your baseball caps, but on speech day, sport caps are rarely in fashion. Of course, like everything else, there are exceptions. If you normally wear a hat and it's part of your signature look, go for it because *you* can rock it. Anything that we wear most of the time becomes a part of us. How many people wear a ring on a different finger as a reminder to do something? The reason why that works is because putting a ring on a different finger feels funny, and that funny feeling reminds us of the task. Similarly, if you're not used to wearing hats, why start on speech day? Just like the ring, it will periodically take your attention away from the task at hand.

Looking Like Champagne on a Beer Budget

We're not telling you all of this so that you run out and spend a fortune on clothes. These days, a lot of offices are pretty casual, especially in the tech and entertainment fields, so your wardrobe could be limited. Or you might be a student or recent graduate on a budget. You might not even own a suit or business dress. That's okay; don't panic. Borrow from a girlfriend or a buddy. Maybe splurge on nice pants, but recycle a dress shirt. Get creative. There are some amazing consignment shops and second-hand stores with designer duds. Just don't wait until the last minute. The truth is that it's actually much more about the intention than anything else. The effort alone is usually enough to win over an audience, especially if they know you as a "jeans and sneakers" guy, but you roll up in a navy blazer and a sharp, Oxford button-down.

You also want to make sure that your clothing is functional and that it doesn't impede your performance. If you've ever worn new leather shoes for the first time, you know what we're talking about. New heels can also be slippery, so you need to wear down the soles to get a little traction. Break them in before your speech day. If you're not used to wearing a tie, try wearing one for an hour just around the house. Practice in it so you're used to the feeling of being choked while trying to give an amazing speech. Sorry, for those of us who don't wear ties on a daily basis, that's pretty much what it feels like. But hey, it's better to get used to it now than experiencing it for the first time on speech day. If you plan to wear a jacket, slip it on and run your speech. Tailored coats can restrict arm movement, so your "gesturing" range of motion might be very different when wearing the jacket than not. Again, better to know now.

Jewelry can be great, but can also have the potential to be a distraction for both you and the audience. Dangling earrings can get caught in hair or mic headsets. Loose bracelets or heavy watches can clink and clang on a podium every time you move. Necklaces can get caught in lavaliere mic packs. Unless you're the Duchess of Windsor, the rule for jewelry is to keep it simple.

The bottom line with wardrobe: Err on the conservative side when choosing your look. Avoid big logos or any clothing with sayings, unless it fits your role, the event, and your audience. Your outfit should never say more than you do.

Smiles Are Always in Fashion

Lastly, our one piece of fashion advice that won't cost you a penny: when in doubt, pull your smile out. Okay, even if you're not in doubt, pull out your smile. A number of studies have shown the benefits of flashing our pearly whites.[5]

Here are some of the ways your smile will save you on speech day:

- It will make you better looking: It is a scientific fact that we are attracted to people who smile.
- They're contagious: If you smile, the whole room will smile back.
- It will warm up the room in an instant: A great grin will defrost the tension in you and everyone else.
- It will put you in a good mood: Smiling releases endorphins and serotonin in your brain, which are the natural "feel good" chemicals.
- It calms you down: Stress can show on your face and smiling relaxes your facial muscles.

Zipping It All Up

This chapter was dedicated to help you pick out the best outfit to wear when giving your speech. We pointed out different things to consider when walking into your closet on speech day (actually, make sure you choose your outfit well in advance, at least by the night before). Be aware of what your clothes are communicating to others, sense how you feel when wearing certain clothes, and choose accordingly. Make sure you've done a test run on any new duds, threads, garb, get-up, apparel, or kicks. Select your outfit to fit the venue and when it doubt, err on the conservative side. But remember, whatever you choose should dress up your confidence. And don't forget to wear your smile, because attitude trumps everything. No one knows if you're feeling nervous or stressed out unless you tell them. So don't tell them! Instead, flash them that beautiful smile.

Try and Apply

Find Your Style

- Evaluate what's in your closet. Take inventory of what you have and what you need.
- What clothes help *you* get in the role of "speech giver"?
- What clothes communicate "I know what I'm talking about"?
- Look for the basics first; leave ties, shoes, and accessories for last.
- Guys: Pick out your suit or nice slacks and shirt combo; solids are always best.
- Gals: Make a decision if you want to wear a dress, skirt, or pants, and choose a shirt to match.
- Try on what you have chosen to make sure it fits and feels good.

- Match your shoes and accessories.
- If you're not sure, ask your friends, the ones that will give you an honest opinion.

Know Your Venue

- Make sure you know at what kind of event or venue you will be speaking so you familiarize yourself with the dress code.
- Find out what kind of people will be there. Who are you speaking to?
- Jot down the articles of clothing that you might need given your research.

Key Notes

1. Clothes communicate: Figure out the image you want your audience to develop about you and dress accordingly.
2. Enclothed cognition: Pay attention to how you want to feel on speech day and dress the part.
3. There are many ways to dress the part, even if you don't own "speech gear" yet.
4. When in doubt, smile!

Chapter 9
Rewire Your Routines

He who is not courageous enough to take risks will accomplish nothing in life.

—Muhammad Ali

Chapter Focus
The secret life of habits.
Rituals, routines, and the feedback factor.

The Secret Life of Habits

Do you have a favorite treadmill at the gym? How about a special spot at the coffee shop? So what happens when you find a total stranger treading on your track or an interloper lounging like he's the freakin' King of England at your table? Sure, there are other treadmills and plenty of empty tables, but that's hardly the point now, is it? Even in these very public spaces, someone is in *your* spot. Sound at all familiar? In the light of day, these habits might appear both quirky and nonsensical, but we're actually programmed for this practice. In other words, we're hardwired to create habits.

As the old adage goes, we're creatures of habit. We love them, we can't get enough of them, and each of us have thousands. It's part of our primitive brain's Department of Defense, protecting us from wandering too far away from the familiar. When our ancestors learned something that was good for them (or at least not fatal), they repeated this behavior over and over. It kept them alive or at least alive a little longer. Still does. Some habits become so habitual that we don't even realize we are doing them. When was the last time you consciously remember putting on your seatbelt? Or, for our nail-biters out there, how often do you notice chewing on your fingers? The benefit of habit forming has also helped humans in a fashion our forbearers could never have fathomed.

Just a few decades ago, your not-so-distant relatives were riding around town in a horse and buggy. Let us repeat that: a horse, buggy, riding around. Today, space tourism is a reality and this extraordinary advance in technology isn't slowing down. In fact, according to research conducted by Gordon Moore, cofounder of Intel, it's growing exponentially.[1] His famed "Moore's Law" says computer-processing speed alone is doubling every 18 months. So how are we able to keep up with all these ever-updating, potentially mind-boggling changes? In part, it's due to our brain's ability to form habits. Habits allow us to absorb and adjust to new information relatively rapidly, creating shortcuts that make most of our daily routines a no-brainer.

Charles Duhigg's book *The Power of Habit: Why We Do What We Do in Life and Business* explains how it works.[2] He argues that every habit starts with a psychological pattern called a "habit loop," which has three parts: a *cue*, which triggers a *behavior* and leads to a *reward*. Habits are shaped when our brains are repeatedly triggered by an experience and we learn to adjust our behavior in such a way that it becomes automatic. For example, as a child, when you first learned to brush your teeth, it took a lot of mental energy, not to mention coaching and modeling behavior from an adult. You might have received praise (reward) for polishing your pearly whites, or at least not scolded for avoiding it. But soon, the behavior of brushing your teeth became routine and now you don't even think about it. Your brain goes into behavior autopilot when it's triggered with the "brush your teeth cue." You've done it every day for years. No mental stress, no cavities. As we mentioned in Chapter 7, teeth brushing has gone from your thinking brain, the prefrontal cortex, to a deeper part of your brain, the basil ganglia.

Of course, we all know that not all habits are productive or good for us. Some routines are just plain rotten. You can tell the difference between the good and the bad by whether they harm us, or someone else, for that matter. And this is where our brain's ability to form habits moves into superstar status, because habits can change. Yes, remember you *can* teach an old dog new tricks. We might be hardwired to have them, but it doesn't mean we can't rework the wiring.

Let's say you have a habit of playing video games every night after you finish your homework. However, you can't just play one game, so it causes you to stay up late. This habit leaves you groggy for your 8 a.m. class and the practice isn't doing you any academic favors. Yet, you still do it. Why? Duhigg argues that in order to break a habit loop, you need to figure out the cue (trigger) and the reward for the particular behavior. Using the example of your late-night video gaming, you may think the cue is finishing your homework and the reward is the excitement of playing video games. In fact, the cue or trigger might be boredom and playing video games is just a way to not be bored (the reward). However, playing video games always leads to late nights, so what else can you do to bust your boredom that won't affect your academics? Why not hit the gym, talk to a friend on the phone, or start your bedtime routine early? In other words, any behavior you do right after you finish your homework will banish the boredom. This will break the habit of staying up late because of the addictive quality of video games. Play them on the weekend! So, understanding the cue and the reward is vital to changing the behavior, which will in turn break the habit.

When it comes to public speaking, many of us have the same destructive habit loop. It starts with the cue, in this case "nerves," and culminates in a behavior: running away as fast as possible. You might be shocked at the number of students who hop huge hurdles just to avoid taking a public speaking class. Other students freely admit they've dropped out of one, two, or even three speech classes because they were too freaked out to finish. Businesspeople will confess they have run from public speaking opportunities their entire career. All of these behaviors lead to a reward: the reduction of anxiety. In many cases, what makes this a harmful behavior is that it limits your potential. At work, this could even mean sacrificing promotions and pay increases.

Whether you realize it or not, you've already begun to break your damaging public speaking loop. Reading this book is a sign that you're tired of running and ready to make a change. It's probably because you recognize that avoiding public speaking is only a temporary fix. You also know that there is a bigger reward at stake. So let's replace your running behavior with these practical alternatives:

- Watch great public speaking videos so it is not such a mystery. The Appendix will point out some great speeches for you to take a look at. Focus on how you feel while you're watching. What is catching your attention? What made their message so inspiring?

- Make it a habit to speak up at work, book club, or any other public forum you may be involved in.

- Begin to really pay attention and listen to how people talk, including yourself. This will help make you aware of which words we use and how we use them to get our message across.

- Conquering your fear of public speaking will give you the courage to face other challenges that may come up in your life.

Flying Through Customs

Both *routines* and *rituals* can become habits; however, they are quite different. A routine is something that is usually well thought out and serves a purpose. For example, if you want to stay in shape, you may run or go to the gym before work at 7 a.m. This usually becomes a routine and something you do, say, every Monday, Wednesday, and Friday. It's based on reality: Exercise equals staying fit.

A ritual, on the other hand, is about associations made in the brain and can have absolutely no rhyme or reason. They can be two unrelated things that have been paired together because the result was favorable or comforts us.

If you're from Philly, you know what the late Kate Smith means to the Philadelphia Flyers. In fact, the hockey team erected a statue of the singer after her death. It all started in the 1960s when Flyers' management piped in a recording of Smith singing "God Bless America" and the team won.[3] The times when it wasn't played, the team lost. Thus, Smith's rendition of Irving Berlin's famous song soon became the Flyers' good luck charm. The Flyers eventually invited Smith to visit Philadelphia and sing live, which she happily did many times. Every time she sang, the Flyers won, including back-to-back Stanley Cups. This pattern continued: Smith sang, the Flyers won; she didn't, they lost. Yes, there were exceptions, but remarkably, to this day, the odds are much greater that the Flyers will win if they play a video of Smith singing her signature song.

Closer to home, we're pretty sure you know someone who believes that if they don't wear their lucky hat or jersey, their team is more likely to lose. The ritual begins, just like in the Flyers' example, when one act is associated with another and it translates into something good or bad. It's a psychological phenomenon.

If we believe in a ritual, we are more likely to ignore the evidence against it and rationalize away the inconsistencies.[4] This has the potential to create a self-filling prophecy. If the Flyers' players believed that they would win if Smith sang, it erased all doubt in their mind and they played to win. Additionally, rituals can comfort us. Believing we have some kind of control in an unpredictable world can relieve stress. Rituals can also be helpful in that they can slow our busy lives down, if just for a moment. For example, there are a few ways to make coffee at home. You can make instant (just add water and stir), use a coffee maker, or even a French press. Our friend Sandra refuses to acknowledge that instant coffee exists in the universe. She also doesn't own a traditional coffee maker. To be clear, Sandra is not what you'd call a coffee snob. For her, it's about the ritual of preparing the coffee that she enjoys the most. She heats the water on the stove (not the microwave), grinds the beans, and then uses a French press. She says that the process, although it takes a few minutes longer to prepare and clean up, forces her to slow down her day, if only for those few moments. Sandra swears the coffee tastes better and researchers say she's probably right—it tastes better to *her*.

Studies conducted have shown that "eating" rituals like singing "Happy Birthday" and blowing out the candles can change our perception of the food itself. In other words, the cake will taste better because we've gone through the ritual.[5] Talk about comfort food!

Clearly, most rituals are harmless. Our rituals only get in the way when our belief in their inevitability creates a damaging, self-fulfilling prophecy. On the days Smith didn't sing, did the Flyers skate onto the ice unsure of their chances? Could this account for the losses? And what about their opponents? What if they also believed Smith had some kind of magical effect on the outcome? If so, how would this affect their playing? It might. In effect, it doubled-down everyone's belief that the outcome was inevitable. So, as long as a ritual doesn't derail you (or throw you off track if you don't do it), it can be an incredible ally.

How can you use the benefits of routines and rituals to prepare you for your big speech? Did you notice any of your own as you were reading this section? If so, what are they? Do you need that cup of coffee to start the day? At night, can you slip into silent slumber only after you're checked your Facebook? Okay, these aren't going to help you on speech day. What will are routines or rituals that calm you down, get you focused, and are associated with your public speaking process. Come up with a routine that you always do as you prepare for your public speaking debut. Our Try and Apply section will help you get started.

Taking Friendly Fire

Feedback is essential to growing as a speaker, but it usually means pitting our yearning to learn against our longing to be liked. In other words, we need the feedback, yet we don't want to hear or heed it. This makes giving and receiving feedback a communication minefield. However, once you understand how our brain functions with feedback, you will be able to eliminate the typical tangles people face, attracting only the advantages.

Think back to the last time you got feedback from a performance, project, or paper. You probably received several very encouraging comments. Yet, we bet you didn't listen to these as loudly as the *negative* notes. It's normal. In fact, research shows that there are separate circuits in our head for positive or negative information.[6] Moreover, we have a negativity bias in our brain; we focus more on our losses than gains. Additional studies conducted by John Cacioppo, a neuroscientist at the University of Chicago, also indicate that electrical activity in our brain spikes higher when encountering negative stimuli than equally powerful positive ones.[7] But why does our brain favor bad news over good?

Have we mentioned it's all about survival? We need to remember the negative so we can do something about it. In other words, be prepared when it shows up or recognize it in order to avoid it. Why? In a word, we want to be liked. If you recall from Chapter 1, being liked means being accepted by our group. Our primal fear is being rejected and ejected from the tribe. It's the ancient urge to be included and strong criticism threatens our membership.

All of this assumes feedback isn't further complicated by other factors, including who is giving it and who is receiving it. Let's say the feedback exchange is between spouses. Researchers at Vanderbilt University studied how husbands received advice from their wives on certain issues.[8] When the feedback was on a topic the men knew well, they were more likely to question their wives' motivation, rather than focusing on the content of the message itself. Our own resistance to taking advice might also impede the flow of feedback. This isn't merely being stubborn. It could mean we're a *reactant*. Psychologists say that reactants will unconsciously do the exact opposite of what is asked of them.[9] They'll do this even when asked by someone they love and even if it's against the reactant's best interest. Though this might sound counter-intuitive, for a reactant, it's an automatic response when they feel their autonomy is threatened.

Gosh, who would have thought feedback could be such a fickle pickle? It certainly can be, but it *is* necessary. So here are a few ways to make feedback work for you:

- Be intentional about focusing on the positive. Your brain naturally notes the negative, but you need to balance both so you can get the most accurate read on your evaluator's response.
- Always assume feedback is coming from an honest and well-intentioned place.

🖋 Keep open. If you resist change without a rational reason, you might be a reactant. In this case, be honest with yourself, careful not to self-sabotage.

Security Blankets: Not Just for Kids

What's on your smart phone screen saver? If you have a photo of someone you love, you wouldn't be alone. Look around your home and office. More photos of people you care about. This isn't a new concept. The tradition of carrying a photo, letter, or lock of hair belonging to a loved one goes way back. In a very real way, these are grown-up security blankets. And according to psychologist Bruce Hood from University of Bristol[10], we carry them around for a couple of reasons. First, there's the sense of nostalgia we feel with objects that were given to us by our favorite teacher, a grandparent, or any person who is special to us. Second, we also develop an emotional attachment to objects. According to Hood, it is called "essentialism," which basically means that there is more to an object than just what they are physically. Don't believe us? Imagine losing that necklace your parents gave you when you graduated high school. Would replacing it with the same exact one *feel* the same? Could you wear a shirt you knew belonged to the notorious serial killer Ted Bundy? Why? According to Hood, it's because we assign an emotional value to objects. Security blankets or special *tokens* also help create comfort when we are in new or unusual situations.

We always encourage speakers to carry or wear something that provides them with a sense of security. These objects need not be visible to the audience; in fact, we hope they're not. As long as the speaker knows he or she has it close to them, it will serve to provide some comfort.

Our friend Vanessa always had her daughter's photo with her when giving a speech and would look at it right before speaking. It made Vanessa feel great, but also reminded her of her responsibility as a mom. Doing one's best in all things (even scary ones) was a lesson she wanted to teach her daughter. And there was no better way to instill that lesson than to live by example. So bring that token with you, knowing that the reason it makes you feel comforted is because you're human!

Closing the Loop

Understanding why we are creatures of habit takes the mystery out of them and will help you get down to business. Do you have a *bad* habit that is getting in your way of delivering your speech *or* do you need to develop a *good* habit to help you deliver your speech? Either way, you now have the tools to tackle both. Developing a routine that gets you in the speech-giving mood can also be essential. Feedback is a very helpful tool that can show you what you need to hone in on and spend a little more time practicing and what you already do well. It is important to give both positive and negative feedback the same weight and attention, as both are very valuable information. Notice if you tend to focus on the negative, and purposefully remind yourself of the positive feedback as well to balance it out. Spend some time looking for that token that helps you feel comforted. Don't worry if you don't have one, you can make one up. Is there anything in your home that has that effect on you? Remember that it has to be small. The main purpose is that when you look at it, it makes you feel comforted, confident, makes you smile, or inspires you in some way.

Try and Apply

Identify the Habits That Don't Serve You

Write down the habits that you recognize in your life. Which ones serve you and which ones not so much? See if you can identify the cue, the behavior, and the reward of the habits you'd like to break. Keep in mind that the cue may not be what you think it is, so dig deeper. Once you have discovered the cue and reward, come up with three alternative behaviors that offer you the same reward.

Create a Public Speaking Ritual

The key to create winning routines is to make sure they work for you and not the other way around. They should be mobile, private, and simple:

- **Make it mobile:** Create a routine you can take on the "road." In other words, something you can do anywhere. For example, pick a theme song that symbolizes your empowered journey as a public speaker. Play it every time you sit down to work on your speech or in the car on your way to give it. If you're in a public space, you can listen to it with headphones on a mobile device. Or, choose a mantra or motto. One of our students used "Eye of the Tiger." Not the music; she just said the phrase before practicing and right before giving her speech (out in the hall or restroom). This incorporates that positive self-talk we learned about earlier. She even made a "tiger's claw" hand gesture when saying it. Either playing or saying your ritual will now be associated with public speaking, and give you confidence and comfort. Additionally, you can incorporate the "Straight From the Horse's Mouth" warm-up you learned as the first step in your new ritual. This will serve as a bonus because it gets your mouth ready to move!

- **Keep it private:** It's personal. If possible, the ritual should be experienced in a safe, quite place. The idea is for you to center and stay focused on the task at hand, without distractions. Besides, it might avoid awkward stares while you're doing the tiger's claw or shouting "Eye of the Tiger." We're just saying.

- **Super simple:** Your ritual need not be a big production or take a lot of time. In other words, you don't need to listen to your theme song the entire time you're working; rather, just to launch you into the mood.

Find Your Security Blanket

As you now know, we can attach emotions to objects. Find a small object that gives you a sense of safety, calm, or confidence that you can carry with you on speech day. Make sure it's something you can easily slip into your pocket or clip inside your shirt, pant, or skirt. Knowing you have it on you will give you a little extra comfort.

Key Notes

1. Habits are automatic behaviors we are mostly unaware of doing.

2. Figuring out what triggers the habit and the reward for doing it will help you change the behavior.

3. Develop a good routine or ritual around your speech practice.

4. Feedback is your friend. Ask for it and learn from it to make your speech the best it can be.

5. Security blankets or tokens help create comfort when we are in new situations; bring one with you on speech day.

Chapter 10
Putting It All Together

It takes one hour of preparation for each minute of presentation time.

—Wayne Burgraff

Chapter Focus
Seven steps to writing your speech.

Getting Started

Whether you have a few days or several months to prepare your big talk, we want you to think small. What we mean is: Don't get ahead of yourself. Thinking about "everything" right now is unproductive, not to mention crazy-making. And you don't have to do it. In fact, it's better if you take this journey in short strides, not long gaits. We've compartmentalized these strides into seven manageable steps. Each step prepares you for the next one and gets you closer to an amazing speech. So, let's get going!

Step One: Hunting and Gathering

Whatever the occasion or topic, you're going to have to gather some intel. We call this *hunting and gathering* because that's what you're doing. Whether giving a best man's toast, keynote, class speech, or commencement address, you need information, lots of it. Of course, the type of speech will determine the kind of information you're after; but no matter, this is the step when you cast a wide net and find out as much as you can about your topic. Don't worry about how you're going to use or structure this information. The focus right now is only on finding information.

In almost all cases, this means an Internet search. Go wide. Look for journal articles, videos, radio interviews, poems, quotes, statistics, and human interest stories. If your topic is personality-driven, like a wedding anniversary or eulogy, you'll also want to interview friends and relatives for stories, anecdotes, and facts. Spend at least a couple of days rifling through records, fingering through family albums, and discovering data. Keep in mind that low-hanging fruit is easier to pick, but often the juiciest and tastiest prizes require more of a stretch. You're not just looking for information that is common knowledge or familiar to your audience; you need to be able to share unique or new information. If not, you'll just be telling them things they already know, and what's the point of doing that? It would be like giving a speech on apples with just the most basic facts. You tell your audience apples are a popular edible fruit, Washington State is famous for them, and we use them in many kinds of dishes, including apple pie. All of these points are true, but this won't surprise (or interest) anybody. But what if, along with this core information, you also shared these delicious facts?

- Today, 11 varieties of apples account for 90 percent of apple production in the country and about five types are sold in supermarkets.
- In the 1800s, there were 7,100 different varieties of apples grown in the United States.
- 86 percent of those apple varieties are now extinct.
- Extinction matters because "crop diversity" is important to our very survival.
- The Svalbard Global Seed Vault in Norway preserves and safeguards almost 900,000 different seed samples from around the world, including existing apple varieties. This helps to ensure future crop diversity.

Did you just learn something? Even if you didn't, chances are still pretty good your average audience will. On the surface, talking about apples sounds like a recipe for yawns, but stretching your search can turn up some intriguing and relatable intel that will attract and maintain your audience's attention.

Step Two: Divide to Conquer

Once you've hunted and gathered far too much information for just one speech (or even three), it's time to divide what you've discovered into themed categories. We use *categories* in this step because it's something our brain has been doing unconsciously since we were babies. And, quite frankly, if our noggin weren't so good at processing and sorting incoming data, we'd be in big trouble.

Several studies have looked at how many advertising and marketing messages Americans are exposed to on a daily basis. Based on what constituted as a message or "exposure," researchers say we're being bombarded by 5,000 messages a day through every medium imaginable including TV, Internet, billboards, store signs, and radio.

That's a marked increase from the 1970s, when urbanites were absorbing 500 every day.[1] With this dramatic increase, why haven't humans gone totally bonkers?

The answer is that our mind is amazing at categorizing everything from sounds to objects. This natural function allows us to navigate the world. Every time we encounter something, we look for what is new, what might be different, and perhaps what has evolved. We make decisions based on the information already stored in our categories and then we update categories based on what we learn.[2]

For instance, as a small child, the first time you heard a smoke detector go off, it might have shocked the hair off your head. Not only was it loud and scary, you weren't sure what it meant for you. Run? Hide? Play dead? Your mind instantly went through thousands of categories to see if this new noise correlated with anything you'd encountered before. No, it wasn't the toilet flushing. It wasn't the sound of your mom's voice, either. It sounded a little like your older brother's alarm clock, but that wasn't a perfect match. Once you learned that it was a smoke detector, you took in this new information and put this new sound and its associations into a category. So, the next time a smoke detector went off, your brain accessed that category, interpreted it, and made an informed decision on what you should do next. As humans, collecting categories allows us to save an enormous amount of time and energy.

So let's put this extraordinary natural inventory system to work. By now you have a general idea of the kind and types of information you've gathered. In fact, your brain has already made some observations, identified patterns, and probably sorted some of the information already. Now, it's time to do this classification intentionally.

What are some of the major themes emerging from your research? Don't worry if you move things around or change your categories a few times. It's part of the process. Experiment a little. Whether you keep everything in separate digital files or go old school with paper piles, just make sure your system allows for flexibility. The number of categories you create depends on how broad or specific you want to make them.

Whereas you might separate your research into two categories, another person might want to create more specific ones. For example, pretend you're preparing a class speech on Canada from the information you've found. You divide your categories into:

1. Historical Canada

2. Modern Canada

Using the same information, another person might divide her categories this way:

1. Pre-Colonization and First Nation Peoples

2. Colonization by England

3. Colonization by France

4. Canada and the American Revolution

5. The Confederation

6. Wars

7. The Canada and Constitution Acts

8. Geography

9. Official Languages

10. Government

11. Food

12. Traditions

13. Olympic History

14. Business and Economy

15. Currency

16. Official Symbols

17. Nicknames and Stereotypes

If you're giving a speech honoring an individual, the same process applies. Say you've been asked to speak at your great-grandfather's

100th birthday. After hunting and gathering, you decide to create the following categories:

1. Childhood
2. Funny Stories
3. Military Service
4. Marriage
5. Family Fishing Trips
6. Best Advice He's Given Each Grandchild
7. Building the Cabin
8. Starting the Family Business
9. How Much Things Cost 100 Years Ago (gas, a loaf of bread, house, etc.)

Whether you have two categories or 200, the important thing is they work for you, not the other way around. You need to keep track of a lot of information and the faster you can locate it, the more time and effort you save. Our advice is you err on the side of more categories than less, and you'll see why when we get to Step Three.

Step Three: The Shape of Things to Come

Now it's time to step back and take a look at what you have. If the answer is "a lot," that's a good thing. But, obviously, you need to make some decisions about what goes in your speech and what won't. You need to start shaping your message. What do you want to say? How do you want to say it? These five questions will help you shape up fast.

What information must absolutely go in the speech?

This includes basic facts the audience will need to know to understand your topic or what they will expect you to share. For example, in the speech on Canada, it would be necessary to say where this country is located in relation to where the audience lives. Or, if you were feting your great-grandpa, you would need to give his current age (100) and other basic facts about his life.

What information is most unique, funny, or surprising?

This is information that is not common knowledge to your audience, but also interesting. For instance, you might say that most Americans might not realize that Canada has a monarchy, a family who is even known to wear crowns and robes once in a while. Or, if it's about great-grandpa, you'll probably hear a lot of interesting anecdotes or discover a lot about him that you and most of the family didn't know. So, if he once caught a whopper of a trout and found a gold watch inside its stomach, that's a good story. But if it was actually a watch he had lost five years before, that's even better. Whatever it is, stories of this kind really make speeches memorable.

What information is most relevant to this audience and occasion?

This is the question that brings your topic "home" for the audience. It's the WIFM (what's in it for me?) question, or in this case, what's in it for the audience? Why should they listen or care about your topic? In your speech on Canada, when speaking to an American audience, you might give examples of how Canadians have helped Americans when they needed it most. For instance, Ken Taylor, the Canadian ambassador in Iran, hid a group of Americans in his home during the 1979 Iranian hostage crisis, a story retold in the Oscar-winning film *Argo*. Or, on September 11, 2001, after the United States closed its airspace, Canada welcomed 239 U.S.–bound flights with 33,000 passengers at 17 airports. Then, entire communities fed and housed those passengers for days and even weeks until they could safely travel to the United States.

For great-grandpa, it would be important to acknowledge the family. How many children, grandchildren, and great-grandchildren does he have?

What overall message do you want to convey in this speech?

This is the primary point of your speech. It's the essence of what you want to say about the topic. Looking at the speech on Canada, maybe it's to point out to the audience that Americans should know more about our greatest ally and neighbor to the north.

For your great-grandpa's speech, it might be to celebrate a humble man who has made a big, positive, and lasting impact on the world.

How do you want the audience to feel about your topic after you're finished speaking?

This question might sound a bit like the previous one, but it's not. The previous question has to do with what you want to *say*; this question is what you want your audience to *feel*. A feeling is an emotional quality and gives you some direction on how you might create and manage your speech's tone to achieve the desired feeling. That being said, you want to make sure they complement each other. In the case of the speech on Canada, the goal is to encourage this audience to know more about their neighboring country. So you might start out your speech by testing the audience's knowledge, proving the point that typical American audiences know very little about Canada. Then, you toss in a few unique facts like Canada's monarchy. And by the way, the Queen of Canada is Queen Elizabeth II, who also independently reigns in England. Your final remarks might highlight how a Canadian crowd recently finished "The Star-Spangled Banner" when the guest singer's mic went out, showing how Canadians know our national anthem, but we probably don't know theirs. And, they're cool enough to sing it. Finally, you might close with the story about how Canadians rescued thousands of Americans on 9/11. In this format, you've set different tones throughout. It's a roller coaster of emotion, but that's good. If done well, you will have accomplished your goal.

For great-grandpa's speech, it would be important to blend humor with touching moments that highlight how humble he is, while sharing how he has made the world a better place for his family and community. Perhaps he served in World War II, but he never talked about it. But then your aunt was going through some old boxes in the attic and discovered he'd won a Bronze Star, something the family and not even his wife knew about. That is pretty typical of that generation of warriors. They did their job and didn't brag about it. On his 100th birthday, it's time to brag on his behalf. The fact that he's never talked about it shows how humble he is, but earning it shows that he served his country and helped bring an immoral dictator to his knees. After the war, he came home, packed up the Bronze Star in a box, and opened a small grocery store. In your research, perhaps you discovered that for more than 40 years he secretly gave groceries on credit to families when they fell on hard times. He did this quietly, without fanfare, and sometimes at a loss to his own business. It's time to tell that story. Again, the "humble helper" theme is illuminated in this powerful tale.

Now it's your turn. Hopefully, we've given you some sparks to fire up your own ideas. Go back and start at the first question. Then take some time to carefully answer all the questions. Take notes as you go. Don't spend too much time thinking or planning ahead. Your only job right now is to tackle these questions as specifically as possible. Remember to refer to your categories regularly. You might even go back and review an article, statistic, or video to refresh your memory.

Step Four: Write Your Headline

The next time you surf the Web, take a look at how many headlines populate the Websites you visit. From search engines to CNN, they are everywhere. All these headlines could be overwhelming, but usually not. As we already learned, your mind is constantly categorizing headlines and making decisions based on your past experiences. Journalists and editors realize this on some level and understand that creating hot headlines is vital to generating traffic and engaging readers.

We want you to write a *headline* for your speech. A headline in a speech is often called a thesis statement. Just like a news headline, it's short, it's direct, and tells the audience the focus of your topic. Unlike news headlines, written after the article is finished, we write the headline before the speech is composed. This is because a speech headline serves a dual purpose. Yes, we use it in the speech to tell the audience the purpose of your speech, but it also tells *you* the focus of your speech. This is a terrific way to stay on track when you're putting it together.

Step Three helped you begin to zero in on what you want to talk about or the message you want to share. But it's probably still a bit of a jumble, so we need to prune and polish it. To show you how this is done, we're going to help our friend Michelle, who's giving a speech on French cooking for a community center's "International Day."

Michelle has spent quite a bit of time on Step One, and she's hunted and gathered a bunch of information. It's far too much for the 15 minutes she's been allotted for her speech. When we meet, she's also completed Step Two by conquering her information and dividing it into 11 categories. They are:

1. French holidays.
2. French films about food.
3. Famous French chefs.
4. French wine.
5. French food.
6. History of French cooking.
7. French table settings.
8. French cooking around the world.

9. Julia Child's impact on French cooking.

10. French cookery books.

11. French cooking schools.

We're also happy to learn that she's taken a couple of days to answer those five questions in Step Three. Here are some of the notes she took:

Well, there seems to be a theme about being intimidated by French cooking. Julia Child was the first to really bring it into average homes through television, but ordering in restaurants might still pose a challenge for some. My goal is to give the audience enough information so they won't be intimidated when ordering in a fancy French restaurant. In other words, they'll know what to expect.

- *I must cover some basic info on French dining.*

- *My speech is about French cooking—must talk about food!*

- *Julia Child demystified French cooking for Americans (relevant to this American audience, well-known personality).*

- *I want the audience to have an understanding of classic French courses so they can order in a fancy restaurant without being embarrassed.*

Michelle has done so much preliminary work; we're able to start crafting her headline right away. Using the notes she brought with her, Michelle wrote a headline that we all agreed was a good start. It narrowed the purpose of her speech to a few short lines:

"Today, I will tell you about how various French dining courses work so that you will want to try French food, and continuing in the tradition of the great Julia Child who popularized French cooking in America, you won't be scared the next time you go to a fancy French restaurant because you're not sure how to order."

However, Michelle didn't *write out loud*. When she tries to say it out loud, she realizes it is really word-heavy, and clunky, and has several different thoughts crammed into one sentence. She also used the word *French* four times in one sentence. It's time to get out the pruning shears. We ask her if she's decided on the purpose of the speech. She tells us that it's really about people being less scared to try fine French dining. So, we suggest that she reorder her two main ideas, putting the "scare" first and "learning" second. Switching these two thoughts automatically makes her headline more audience-centered and states her purpose first. The emphasis is now on helping the audience by teaching them what they need to know.

Here's what Michelle comes up with next:

"Today, I want to take the intimidation out of fine French dining by introducing you to the various courses that make up a classic French meal."

It sounds pretty good to us, and she had really pruned wordiness. She's also correct to take out the mention of Julia Child. There wasn't any need to mention Child because the speech isn't about this famous American chef; it's on French dining. Michelle will still talk about Child in her speech, of course. Now that the clutter is removed from the headline, we can see another opportunity to prune. This is Michelle's final headline:

"Today, I want to take the intimidation out of fine French dining."

What happened to the "various courses" line? Michelle decided her purpose is really to take the intimidation out of fine French dining. She's going to do so by introducing the courses. And though she'll probably spend more time speaking about the courses, the *purpose* of doing so is to make fine French dining less scary.

There's a great reason to be really strict with your headline. The more focused your headline, the easier it will be to organize and stay on track while you're writing your speech. One of the many benefits (and we'll share others later) of a tightly written headline is that it tells you exactly what information to include in your speech, and what information (even if super interesting) doesn't fit.

Step Five: Crowd Control

Now that you have your headline, go back and take a look at all of your categories. Using your headline as a guide, separate the categories that apply from those that don't. Be tough. You're only interested in categories that will help support your headline. Set aside everything else. If you're unsure about a category, keep it in the mix until you can figure out if it works or not.

The goal here is to cut your categories down significantly. By significantly, we mean wean them down to two or three. Yes, we're serious. If you have to consolidate categories, do so, but clean out any information you can't use to make it easier for you to access later.

What does this look like in practice? Let's go back to Michelle's French cooking speech. She had 11 categories to start. And here's her headline:

"Today, I want to take the intimidation out of fine French dining."

First, we eliminate categories that do not directly support this headline. Let's cross them out.

1. French holidays.
2. ~~French films about food~~
3. ~~Famous French chefs~~
4. French wine
5. French food
6. History of French cooking
7. French table settings
8. ~~French cooking around the world~~
9. Julia Child's impact on French cooking
10. ~~French cookery books~~
11. French cooking schools

Our new list looks like this:

1. French wine
2. French food
3. History of French cooking
4. French table settings
5. Julia Child's impact on French cooking

Then, let's combine similar categories to create two new ones:

1. The French dining experience
2. Classic French meal courses

These two remaining categories (at the most, three) are going to be your main points. So you've got your headline and main points. Now it's time to organize and outline.

Step Six: Heart of the Parts

How many types of speeches can you think of? There are hundreds, but all speeches have the same basic structure: a beginning, middle, and end. It's a format you know very well because every good story has the same structure. TV shows, films, books, articles, fables, and even stories you tell your friends have this three-point structure. All three must be there or it doesn't work. Imagine reading a fantastic book, one you're really into, and two-thirds of the way in, you find out someone has ripped out the remaining chapters. Do you just shrug and forget about it because you're content with just reading some of the book? We're guessing not so much. Our brain needs all three to complete a story.

A speech outline also has all three of these parts, but we use different names for them. We call the beginning the *introduction*, the middle is called the *body*, and the end is called the *conclusion*. You know this terminology if you've ever had to outline a paper in school. We're going to take you through a basic speech outline and show how you can use it to build your speech. This format will work in most cases, but you might have to tailor it to fit your particular speech. If you've done the previous steps, you should be able to follow this outline from top to bottom and start filling in information next to each bullet point. We don't want to say it's as easy as "fill in the blank," but it's close. Use complete sentences, but *write out loud*. Remember: Always write your speech to be *said*, not *read*.

Introduction

- Write down your headline.
- Write down your first main point.
- Write down your second main point.

Body

- Write down your first main point.
- Write down your second main point.

Conclusion

- Write down your headline.
- Write down your first main point.
- Write down your second main point.

You might be looking at this and thinking, "Why in the heck did I just write the same thing over and over again?" It's because in the introduction you *preview* your **main points**. You don't elaborate; you just share with us how you're going to support your headline by telling the audience what your two main points will be. In the body, elaborate on your main points, and in the conclusion restate your headline and recap your two main points. This might seem like overkill, but it will hold a nice structure for your speech and help your audience follow along.

Moving on, we're going to add a few more bullets to the outline. The first bullet is called *topic overview*. In this section, you give us a snapshot of the topic on a broad scale; it leads into your headline, but it's not the headline itself. One of the easiest ways to write this section is to go back to Step Three and refer to the notes you took when you answered the five questions.

The second bullet is often called a *personal credibility statement.* We're going to call it a *personal* or *professional connection.* It's a few sentences telling the audience why you care about this topic, or what makes you the expert on it. For example, if you are doing a speech on breast cancer, and you have a personal connection to the disease, you might want to share it here. Or, maybe you're a cancer researcher or medical professional. Again, this is where that kind of information goes.

You'll notice, we've also added *sub-points* below each of your main points. As you write, you'll decide what is the best information to include in these sub-points to support your main points. Creating bullets also reminds you to give your main points equal time and emphasis. Along with sub-points, we've added bullets to mark where you'll need *transitional* sentences. These sentences help your audience know, "Hey, we're leaving this section and moving on to the next." A common transitional sentence sounds similar to this: "Now that we've taken a look at XYZ, let's turn our attention to ABC." It's a linking device that bridges one idea to another.

Introduction

- *Write down your topic overview.*
- Your headline.
- *Write down your connection.*
- *Write down your transitional sentence.*
- Your first main point.
- *Write down your transitional sentence.*
- Your second main point.
- *Write down your transitional sentence.*

Body

- Your first main point.
- *Write down your sub-point #1.*
- *Write down your sub-point #2.*

- *Write down your transitional sentence.*
- Your second main point.
- *Write down your sub-point #1.*
- *Write down your sub-point #2.*
- Write down your transitional sentence.

Conclusion

- Your headline.
- Your first main point.
- Your second main point.

Now it's time to book-end your speech. Our hard and fast rule is *always use an attention-getter.* Never, ever start your speech out by telling us what your speech is about. A sentence like, "My speech is about" or "I'm going to give a speech on..." should *never* start a speech. *Ever.* We've mentioned this before, but we can't emphasize it enough. It is akin to revealing the punch line before delivering the joke. So what is an attention-getter? Well, that's easy: It's something that grabs an audience's attention and makes us want to hear a lot more. Attention-getters should relate to your topic and be relatively brief. It's the flirting we discussed in Chapter 5.

Great examples of attention-getters can be funny or serious stories, quotes from important people, a few lines from a poem or song, and even a strange sound. Asking a question to involve the audience is a good way to engage them, but be careful it doesn't turn into a question and answer session. For example, you can start your speech by asking, "How many of you can use an extra $1,000 a month?"

Your attention-getter is one bookend to your speech; the other is what we call the "Big Bang!" This is the last thing you say in your speech. Too often we've heard speakers who don't plan an ending. But the ending is what people tend to remember. Good or bad, it leaves a lasting impression. So what kind of impression will you leave your audience with? Your **Big Bang!** can use the same kind of engagement devices as you use for an attention-getter, but almost everyone gets stuck coming up with a new, relevant one. The good news is that there is a hack for this. Use your attention-getter as the basis for your Big Bang! However you started your attention-getter, finish it in the Big Bang! You don't have to do this literally, but if you refer to it in some way, you will put a natural button on your entire speech. For example, you can end your speech by saying, "Now that you know how you can increase your income by $1,000 a month, you can start dreaming about how you're going to spend it."

We also strongly suggest that you practice your attention-getter and Big Bang! a lot. You should absolutely memorize them. Remember: First and last impressions last longer than anything else in a speech. And if you're looking down and fumbling, reading off an index card or sheet of paper, it dramatically reduces the impact of these critical moments.

Introduction

- *Write down your attention-getter.*
- Your topic overview.
- Your headline.
- Your connection.
- Your transitional sentence.
- Your first main point.
- Your transitional sentence.
- Your second main point.
- Your transitional sentence.

Body

- Your first main point.
- Your sub-point #1.
- Your sub-point #2.
- Your transitional sentence.

- Your second main point.

- Your sub-point #1.

- Your sub-point #2.

- Your transitional sentence.

Conclusion

- Your headline.

- Your first main point.

- Your second main point.

- *Write down your Big Bang!*

Once you've completed your outline, it shouldn't be your final draft. You can now write out a manuscript or keep revising the outline. Just remember to always write out loud.

Step Seven: Stand and Deliver

We're going to be very clear here: You can't *over-practice*. It's impossible. And we guarantee that when you sit down from delivering your speech, or during the car ride home, you will wish you had practiced at least once more, if not a million. Most people practice just a fraction of the time necessary. It's shocking when we hear people say they only practiced their speech a couple of times or just in the car on the way to give it.

Sometimes people will ask us how many times they should practice a speech. There's no definitive answer for this, but if pressed for an actual number, we'll tell them at least 25 times. They are blown away. Then we add that that's just the start. And they have to do it standing up as if they are actually giving it to a real audience. The rest of the time can be in the car, in the shower, or any free second they have. Many people are really put off by this news and usually groan audibly, before reverting back to their original plan of just running it through in their heads a couple of times and then maybe in front of their dog. These are the same people who whine about being "nervous" and are the first to tell you and everyone else that they are "terrible speakers." Yet, they can't be bothered to practice or do something to fix it.

What's the rationale to set oneself up for failure? Is it so they can say, "Well, that proves I'm a terrible speaker"? Or is it because they fear they will practice and still not do well? The fact is that you will *always* do better if you practice, so there is zero chance of winning that argument. You only lose by not practicing. Period.

We realize that for different reasons, everyone cannot practice as much as we believe is necessary, so we took this into account with our write out loud approach. The good news for you is you've been practicing all along. Your advantage right now is time. However, this doesn't mean you're finished and it's suddenly cocktail hour. Nice try. You now kick it into high gear and bring home the gold.

Here are our best practicing practices:

- Stretch out your body before every practice, especially neck and shoulders.
- Warm up your mouth before every practice, no exceptions. Use our Straight From the Horse's Mouth trick in Chapter 7.
- Stand up and practice *out loud* as often as possible.
- Practice as if you're giving the speech to an audience.
- Practice in front of a mirror several times to see your facial expressions and gestures.
- If possible, check out the room you'll be speaking in, walk around, and get the feel for it.
- Understand every single word and be able to pronounce everything correctly.
- Tape yourself (audio/video). This is a scary but necessary experience.

- Run your entire speech in bed, right before you shut your eyes, and when you wake up, run through as much of it as you remember.

- Time yourself! Make sure you're within the time limit and consistent.

- Practice without words to work out your gestures. Memorize and understand every single word and phrase.

- Memorize the attention-getter and Big Bang!

- Practice with your visual aids.

- Visualize success.

- Eliminate all negative self-talk during all practices, no exceptions!

- Shut down your inner critic during all practices, no exceptions!

- Practice every single day, multiple times, if possible.

Make Your Notes Noteworthy

Memorized speeches are always best. They free you up to live in the moment. You can gesture more easily and make real contact. It also shows you have taken the occasion and this audience seriously. The second best strategy is to speak *extemporaneously*. This basically means you have notes with you, but only refer to them periodically. It does not mean that you will be speaking off-the-cuff or making it up as you go. When you speak extemporaneously, you know the basic elements of your speech very well. You have worked out the sentence structure. Your notes are there to keep you on track, not for you to be tied to them.

Barring memorization, you should use *note cards*, a *manuscript*, or an *outline*. But never ever use an electronic device like a smartphone or tablet. *Ever.* There is too much room for error. There are countless reasons for this, but the big one is they aren't meant for speeches.

A young woman who read off her smartphone delivered one of the worst speeches we ever heard. The speech itself was fine, but her delivery was disastrous. She looked down the entire time and scrolled. She would often scroll too far and then have to scroll back. The font was tiny, so she held the screen very close to her face, which covered it during the entire speech. If this weren't bad enough, about half-way through her speech, she started getting text messages. And she actually answered one of them! Talk about distracting for everyone involved.

So, again, our suggestions are old-fashioned note cards, a manuscript, or outline. Whatever you choose, remember this tool is for *you*, not for your audience. In other words, make it you-ser friendly. If you're using a manuscript or outline, use GIGANTIC font, and double space. We're not kidding. It's because when you get up in front of the room, magically, that 12-point font will shrink to 8, and your single-spaced sentences will suddenly look like a giant blob. Okay, it's not magic; it's nerves that make things go wonky on the page. The same goes for note cards: Write big.

Another word of advice: Don't worry about it being neat and tidy. This is your tool, so make notes on it, highlight or underline key words or phrases, draw a smiley face, or do whatever will help you.

In our classes, new students are often afraid to turn in the notes they used for their speeches. It's usually because the pages or note cards are covered in writing or have words crossed out, or the pages are crumpled a bit. What they don't understand is that we love to see these markings. The personal "coding" on their notes mean a student has lived with the document, practiced with it, and used it as a tool to get the job done. A tool is only helpful if it's used. Think about garden tools. If a shovel is shiny and unmarked, it means it hasn't been used. But you can always spot the tools a gardener finds the most helpful, because they look like they've been through World War III.

Visual Aids Should Be Visual and Aid

On some occasions, you'll want to use visual aids. Here are our top tips for using them:

- Avoid using the whiteboard or chalkboard.
- Prepare visual aids in advance.
- Practice with your visual aids.
- Make sure your visual aids are *big enough* for all to see.
- Display visual aids where the entire audience can see them.
- Do not stand in front of visual aids.
- Avoid passing visual aids among the audience.
- Do not give a handout to your audience while you are speaking.
- Display visual aids only while discussing them.
- Talk to your audience, not to your visual aids.
- Explain visual aids clearly and concisely.
- Use your aid during the speech, not after.
- If possible, use a professional slide program like Prezi or PowerPoint.
- *Most importantly, your visual aids are there to support your speech, not distract from it, replace your delivery, or otherwise diminish your own performance.*

Keep Calm and Speak On

Okay, we wouldn't be the least surprised if you're feeling a bit overwhelmed at this point. It's a lot to take in. We tossed a ton of new terminology and theory at you. Then, we turned everything most people believe about public speaking upside down—all of it, just to get to this point where we put it all together. So, if you were considering taking a break until the day before your speech, we wouldn't blame you. But we wouldn't recommend it either.

You can't cram for a speech. There are too many moving parts, and each of them needs to be fine-tuned and then connected with each other. And in public speaking, like in many other things in life, the whole is always greater than the sum of its parts.

If you do decide to put off planning, preparing, and practicing until the very last minute, it is guaranteed not to be as good as if you work on it, even a little, over a longer period of time. Moreover, if you don't do nearly as well as you had hoped, your poor showing will falsely reinforce a belief that you're a bad speaker. But it's not because you're a bad speaker, it's because you didn't invest the time in yourself or your speech to be able to do your best.

Do yourself a favor and fight to be better. First, turn off the inner critic.

Remember your inner critic can be one tricky character, using both sour and sweet nothings to convince you to procrastinate. She could be saying to you right now that you are too stressed out to get started. Or he could sound very reasonable, even complimentary. If you're saying to yourself, "I work best on deadlines, so waiting is actually better for me," that's just sweet talk to slow you down. And just so you know, he'll be the same guy berating you when you're totally unhinged, because you've waited until the last minute. With the inner critic, there's just no winning.

Now that we've settled that, it's Go Time!

Key Notes

1. Step One: Find out as much unique and new information about your topic as you can.

2. Step Two: Break this information down into categories.

3. Step Three: Begin shaping your speech by placing each category in order of importance.

4. Step Four: Write a headline for your speech to focus you on the information that needs to be included.

5. Step Five: Go back to your categories and cut out the ones that don't apply.

6. Step Six: Outline your speech's introduction, body, and conclusion.

7. Step Seven: Practice, practice, practice!

Chapter 11
Speak Easy:
Tips for 7 Types of Speeches

7 Types of Speeches

Impromptu Speaking

You're not always going to have a lot of time to prepare or practice for a speech. In fact, you might only have a few minutes or *less*. This kind of presentation is called an *impromptu* speech. It's those times when someone rushes up to you and says, "Hey, dude, Jason is stuck in traffic. Can you give the toast?" or "We forgot to get someone to introduce the district manager. Can you say a few words?" Though this might seem like a nightmare scenario, it's probably because you think "impromptu" means giving a speech without *any* preparation. And giving a speech without any prior thought would be a bad dream.

Even the highest skilled speakers wouldn't consider this off-the-cuff approach. They know that it's only a recipe for endless rambling in search of a point. Don't gamble with a ramble! You should absolutely prepare because you *always* have time, even if this means collecting yourself and your thoughts in a minute or less. The idea here is to maximize every single second. It's a lot simpler than it sounds, especially because you already know the fundamentals of public speaking: Nerves are good and the audience is not your adversary. So all you have to do the next time an occasion calls for an impromptu speech is Collect, Assess, List, and Make it happen! In a word, C.A.L.M. yourself.

Collect yourself. Acknowledge your anxiety and accept it. Get rid of any negative self-talk. If you are able and have time, find a quiet retreat (even a bathroom stall) to prepare.

Assess the situation. Focus on the job at hand. What have you been asked to do? Be specific. For example, are you introducing a VIP? Perhaps toasting a retiring colleague? How much time do you have to speak? Who is your audience?

List your ideas. Jot down a few thoughts first. Create a simple outline (introduction, body, conclusion) on a piece of scratch paper, the back of a business card, a napkin, or even your mobile phone. Now, think of a great attention-getter, main points, and of course, a great Big Bang!

Make it happen! This is no time to be shy. If you can, do the "Straight From the Horse's Mouth" exercise and, if needed, the "Hat Trick." Run your ritual. If you have time, practice out loud or go over the list in your head as many times as you can. Then get up and show your stuff.

Example:

A couple of years ago, Steve was asked to introduce the on-air Fox News personality Gretchen Carlson to a New York audience. He had about 10 minutes to prepare. He immediately started getting C.A.L.M. First, he acknowledged his nerves and accepted them.

Next, he found a quiet place. In this case, it was a storage closet. It was not exactly glamorous, but a useful place to *Collect* himself. He made sure the organizers knew where to find him and he set his timer on his phone to alert him when he had just a few minutes left. Then, he began to *Assess* the situation. His job was to introduce Carlson to about 400 people, including a few of her family members and friends. He would have about a minute at the most to do it—no easy feat when you're talking about such an accomplished woman. But to this particular audience, Carlson was more than an impressive resume. Steve wanted to show her warmth, sincerity, and heart, too. He knew a few professional and personal facts. For example, he knew Carlson was from Minnesota and had been Miss America. She had been on *Fox & Friends* and now hosted her own show on Fox News Channel. Using this information, he launched his *List* by jotting down a few ideas and then creating an outline: introduction, body, and conclusion. He used his phone to do an Internet search—to make sure he got his details right—and then went to work filling in the outline.

Here's some of what he jotted down on his list:

- Minnesota—nickname "North Star" State.
- True North sounds like North Star.
- Miss America 1989.
- CBS News, *Fox & Friends*, *The Real Story*.
- Faith is important—friends and family in audience.

Then, he created this simple outline:

Introduction

- Attention-getter
- Minnesota/Miss America
- Transition sentence

Body

- Broadcast career (CBS, *Fox & Friends*, *The Real Story*)
- Transition sentence

- 🔊 Gretchen as a person (faith, family, friends)
- 🔊 Transition sentence

Conclusion

- 🔊 Please welcome Gretchen Carlson!

After he had worked out the attention-getter, the Big Bang! and transition sentences, he was ready to *Make it Happen!* He was able to practice out loud a couple of times, stretched out, rolled his neck, and did the "Straight From the Horse's Mouth" trick. Because he used the Write out Loud and Write to be Said, Not Read approach, he had memorized his speech by the time someone came to get him out of "storage."

This was Steve's speech of introduction for Gretchen Carlson that evening:

She hails from the North Star state, the great state of Minnesota. But she would represent all of us when, in 1989, she became Miss America. Yet this was not her first or last crowning achievement.

She soon entered the competitive field of broadcast journalism, first at CBS News and then as a familiar face on Fox & Friends. Today, she hosts her own show, The Real Story With Gretchen Carlson.

Despite her extraordinary success, this daughter of Minnesota never forgot where she came from and her "true north" will always be her faith, family, and friends. Ladies and gentlemen, please welcome Gretchen Carlson.

Whether your impromptu speech is to introduce someone (even yourself) or sell a product, stay C.A.L.M. Above all, don't strive for perfection (you know we're not fans of this goal), but rather be authentic, passionate, and alive in the moment.

Speech of Introduction

Steve's speech for Carlson was an impromptu speech, but also a speech of introduction. These are short speeches welcoming a notable who is going to give a longer speech or presentation. Speeches of introduction should always be two minutes or less. Here are some guidelines as you prepare and practice:

- Research! Find out everything you can about this person. Listen to or watch any interviews you can find. Try to figure out what accomplishments the notable finds most important. Clues can be found in how a host or interviewer introduces them, what their official biography says, and how they answer interview questions. Ignore obscure information unless it is directly relevant to the occasion and audience. Remember: This is to introduce the audience to the speaker, but it should also energize and give the speaker confidence too. So, keep in mind that you need to appeal to two audiences here.

- Memorize your introduction speech. Introductions read off manuscripts or note cards are spirit killers.

- Know how to pronounce the speaker's name, titles, or affiliations (like schools or organizations).

- Do not just list off accomplishments. The audience probably has some familiarity with the speaker and doesn't need to hear a resume. Highlight only achievements that this audience would find most impressive or interesting.

- If necessary, give the audience a very brief overview of what the speaker will be talking about. But avoid giving the "title" of the speech, which is usually dry and way too long.

- This speech isn't about you—at all. It has nothing to do with you, so don't insert yourself—unless you have a very personal connection—and even then, acknowledge it briefly.

- Find a "local connection" between the speaker and audience. Even the slimmest of links can build a bridge.

- Don't forget to invite the audience to welcome the speaker warmly.

Acceptance Speech

If you are nominated for an award *or* know in advance you will be receiving one, do not "wing" your acceptance speech. Some people think it's bad luck to prepare a speech, that it somehow jinxes the process. Good luck with that. All it does is freak you out even more, not to mention disrespects the award and the award-givers.

One of the best acceptance speeches given recently was by actress Viola Davis at the 2015 Primetime Emmy Awards. It was evident that she prepared, and rightly so. Davis clearly understood that if she won, the moment would be historic. Here's why: When her name was called, she became the first African-American woman to win an Emmy for "Outstanding Lead Actress in a Drama Series" in history. To her credit, Davis didn't waste this occasion talking about her career or rambling in search of a point. Instead, she used this golden opportunity as a national platform to call for better lead roles for women of color. In doing so, she made the moment so much bigger than herself and discussion of diversity in Hollywood evolved in an instant.

Thousands of industry folks heard her message and it resonated with millions of television viewers. When it went viral, it reached millions more. People were clearly moved by her message, but probably wouldn't be able to tell you exactly why other than it was authentic, passionate, and almost poetic. As a public speaker, you can see a simple outline: introduction, body, and conclusion. There was also that kick-butt attention-getter (a quote from Harriet Tubman) and a Big Bang! In a word, Davis killed it and you can do it, too. Here are some specific things to think about when preparing an acceptance speech:

- Know how much time you have to give your speech and plan accordingly! If the award show is televised, and you're going over time, you don't want your final remarks drowned out by orchestra music. Even if it's not an issue of airtime, you still want to leave the audience both impressed and wanting more.

- Make it personal and speak from the heart. Tell the audience what winning the award means to you.

- Don't read off a piece of paper or note cards—nothing kills authenticity faster. Looking down the entire time is not an option.

- Avoid long lists of people you want to acknowledge. This distances you from everyone in the room except those people. The exception is if you want to thank someone like a spouse, parent, teacher, mentor, or grandparent who gave you special encouragement.

- Keep it structured! Do not wander off topic; you don't want anyone to regret giving you the award.

Presentation Speech

On the other side of the podium, you might have the opportunity to present an award to someone else. This is an honor in and of itself, so don't take it lightly. Obviously, it's a big deal for the person receiving the award and a moment they will remember for years to come. It's your job to help create a positive, lasting memory. Here are some ideas to keep in mind when preparing a presentation speech:

- Remember you not only represent yourself, but the organization bestowing the award. Don't wait until the last minute to prepare and practice. Yes, you have to practice!

- Describe the award and what it represents. Is it named after someone? If so, who were they and why was this award established? Are there other notables who have received the award? If so, you might consider naming a few.

- Clearly explain why the recipient or organization is receiving the award.

- Know how to pronounce the recipient's name! This is a *must*.

- Know when you'll be speaking and plan accordingly. Go use the bathroom. Warm up your mouth. Don't be late!

- Know where you're going. When it's time to speak, have the route planned out or at least have someone who knows the path guide you.

- Practice at the podium or wherever you'll be standing when presenting the award. Get a sense of the room, microphone, and teleprompter (if applicable). Is the podium so high that you can't see over it? Make sure you have something to stand on. It's better to find out that the audience is only going to see the top of your head before you go up there.

- Know which direction the recipient will be coming from if possible. What area of the room and/or which side of the stage will the recipient enter from? Some evening events will have spotlights on the stage, which can be blinding. Be prepared for this and don't acknowledge it as a problem or challenge. The audience doesn't know you can't see all of them clearly; be the pro and don't bring it up.

- Know where you exit. The recipient will be in your hands after they finish speaking, so be prepared to guide them in one direction or the other. Running back and forth is not a good look.

Toasts and Roasts

A toast is figuratively "raising a glass" in someone's honor. These are usually at celebrations like weddings, anniversaries, or retirement parties. Toasts pay tribute to an achievement or milestone. The best approach is to mix humor with sincerity. Roasts, like toasts, also honor someone, but are always primarily focused on humor. Think of it like "pushing someone's buttons" or "ribbing" someone you like. You aim "below the belt," but in good taste. Here are some additional thoughts on giving toasts and/or roasts:

- Prepare: Research and write down your thoughts.

- Make it personal, but not too "inside baseball." In other words, think of the larger audience and avoid "inside jokes" that only a few people might understand.

- Watch some roasts online. We love the old *Dean Martin Celebrity Roast* series; they're smart and hilarious without getting too down and dirty like the more contemporary ones. Remember: Not everyone appreciates foul language, and you have to think about your audience.

- Make a list of the honoree's special characteristics. These are usually personality traits. For instance, is the person considered a "cheap skate" or "naïve"? Use these as starting points for jokes or to tell anecdotes.

- Consult with other people to get ideas.

- Practice the speech in front of others to get feedback. What's working and what's not?

- For roasts: Think "funny," but act serious. The big rule is that you *always* end the roast speech on a positive note, saying how much you genuinely love and admire the person.

Eulogy or Memorial Speeches

Eulogies are given at memorial services and funerals. Although you and the audience are grieving, this is a time to celebrate life, not death. The audience is looking to you to guide them in how to handle their loss. That's why it's important to stay focused on the job at hand and in control of the moment. Yes, this will be an emotionally charged situation, but that's why planning and practice are critical. Here are a few things to remember when crafting a eulogy:

- It's not about you. How many times have you heard eulogies that are all about the speaker? Too often. Don't do it.

- Acknowledge the immediate family; they are the most deeply affected.

- Tell stories (funny and/or poignant) that highlight the deceased's most special qualities.

- Memorize or speak extemporaneously.

- Keep it short. Chances are good there will be other speakers at the service, so be respectful of those people and the audience.

Commencement Speech

Whether you are an invited commencement speaker or a student speaker, commencement speeches go one of two ways: trite or terrific. There are rarely any kinds in between. Trite speeches are never remembered; terrific speeches can inspire graduates for years to come. Decide which kind of speech you want to give. Assuming it's the terrific type, it's time to avoid clichés and the obvious go-tos. For example, we love Dr. Seuss, but his literature doesn't belong in a graduation speech. Graduates will receive at least a thousand copies of *Oh, The Places You'll Go!* so they don't need to hear it in your speech—please! Here are other tips for a terrific commencement speech:

- Acknowledge the dignitaries, faculty, and other important speakers, and then, finally, the graduates first. This is one of the rare cases when you don't start with an attention-getter because it's tradition to recognize the luminaries first.

- Talk to the graduates. This is where a speech to be said, not read, comes in. Fancy words and long academic phrases will destroy any chance of real engagement with the students. Yes, families, friends, and faculty are in the audience, but this speech is not primarily for them.

- Remember the graduates aren't there for a lecture. In fact, they aren't even sitting there to hear you. They are graduating, and leaving good friends and the only routine they've known for a few years, and facing an uncertain future. They're scared. Your only job is to encourage them, share a few laughs, and point them in the right direction. Stay positive. Okay, so the world is falling apart, but this might not be the time to bring that up unless you make their journey going forward part of the solution.

- Get personal. Use a story or two to illustrate how you got through a tough time or faced an uncertainty.

- Don't settle for crass to get laughs. Clever speakers don't have to resort to crotch humor. If you're a graduating student, your future employer might be sitting out there.

- Don't go too long. Ask ahead of time how much time you will have and stick to it. Commencement ceremonies are notoriously long affairs; don't make it unnecessarily longer. Graduates, friends, and family have "places to go."

Watch and Learn

Improving your skills as a public speaker involves more than just doing it yourself. In fact, seeking out and watching other public speakers is one of the most valuable ways you can improve your own speaking. However, in the past, most of the time you were probably a "passive" listener. Unless you were personally invested in the message (a cause you care about, for example) or speaker (your best friend or sister), chances are good that at some point, your mind drifted and the speech just became background noise for your thoughts. After the speaker wrapped up his or her talk, you did little more than check a mental box. Were you entertained? "Yes," "No," or "Maybe." Whatever the answer, you didn't clearly understand how or why this was the case. You also had no personal reason to care much about the speaker's personal speaking style. After all, why would you?

However, your mission now is to help you improve your own skills as a public speaker. The good news is that it's not going to take a herculean effort on your part; it simply means you'll have to go from being a "passive" listener to an "active" one. "Active listening" is listening with a *purpose* in order to gain information. When it comes to public speaking, the purpose of the "message" is only a fraction of the information you're after. More importantly, given your goal to be a great public speaker, is to stay alert to all of the elements you've learned in *Scared Speechless*: situation, audience, delivery, organization, storytelling, and even attire.

As an active listener you'll gain valuable insight into what works and doesn't for other speakers and why this might be. Ultimately, this information will help guide you as you develop your own speaking persona. When we say "your own," we mean just that. Mimicking another speaker should never be your objective. That being said, we strongly encourage you to experiment with the various delivery aspects of several speakers, but always be mindful that what works for one speaker might look very silly on another.

When actively listening to other speakers, consider recording your observations in a small notepad, paying special attention to aspects of a speaker's style or modes of delivery that you particularly think are effective or not. Now that you've read the book and are familiar with different aspects of preparation and performance, here are several elements of a delivery and personal style you may want to look out for and make note of:

- Did the speaker use an attention-getter? If so, what was it?
- How was his or her speaking rate? Did they talk too fast or really slowly?
- Did the speaker make eye contact with the audience?
- Could you hear the speaker clearly at all times?
- How was the speaker's posture? Did they slouch or fidget?
- Did the speaker tell any stories? If so, were they effective?
- Did the speaker use humor? If so, did it work? Why or why not?
- Was the speaker appropriately dressed?
- Was there anything distracting about what they wore?

- Did the speaker stop for laughs or other responses from the audience?

- Were you distracted by any gestures or body language?

- Did the speaker use visual aids? If so, were they effective?

- If appropriate to the situation, did the speaker smile?

- Did the speaker memorize her speech? If not, did she use notes?

- Do you think the speech was written to be said or to be read?

- How long did the speaker talk? Did it seem too long or too short?

- Did the speaker have a "White Out"? If so, how did he handle it?

- Could the speaker pronounce all of their words correctly?

- Did the audience seem engaged? If so, when were they most tuned in?

- Did anyone walk in or out during the speech? If so, how did the speaker handle this?

- Did the speaker have a Big Bang! in their conclusion?

- Did the speaker seem prepared? Why or why not?

- Do you think the speaker practiced enough? Why or why not?

- How did you feel about the speaker and their message after the speech?

Event Horizon

Although it might seem daunting to find decent public speakers, it's really just a matter of opening up your front door and, perhaps, your mind a little. Here are a few reliable places to hear speakers of all skill levels speak their piece.

- ● **The public library.** Check out your local library. Most will have a calendar of events with speakers of all types (including authors, of course) listed online. These events are free.

- ● **Schools.** If you live near a college or university, public speeches are being delivered all the time by professors, administrators, or visiting scholars. There are usually several different "speaker series," depending on the college or department. These aren't always just for students. In fact, many are open to the public for free or for a small fee.

- ● **Bookstores.** Independent or chain bookstores "book" speakers regularly. These include nationally recognized or local authors who do readings and signings.

- ● **Places of worship.** Speaking isn't just for Saturday or Sunday. Many houses of worship have daily activities, including speakers. Check out local churches, synagogues, or mosques to find out more.

- ● **Forensics (speech and debate).** High schools and colleges across the country compete against each other almost every weekend in about a dozen different individual speaking events as well as several kinds of debate. Individual events include three types: platform (sometimes called public address), limited preparation, and oral interpretation of literature. In platform speeches, speakers typically have about 10 minutes to inform or persuade you on a specific topic of their choosing. Students memorize their speeches and a judge (usually a teacher or professor) critiques them. Limited preparation events can be nail-biters. In these events (impromptu and extemporaneous speaking), students are given a topic (for example, domestic or foreign policy) and only have a limited amount of time to prepare and deliver a speech on that topic to a judge. In oral interpretation of literature, students have

10 minutes to perform a poetry, prose, or drama program for a judge. These events are also memorized, but students might use notes or hold a small black binder with the text. The students will blow you away with their talent! Contact your local school to see if they have a speech program. Then, inquire about tournaments in your area. These tournaments are open to the public and free. The "forensics" community is wonderful about welcoming visitors. Just know that there are a few protocols to follow when observing student speeches. The biggest one is to never walk in or out while a student is speaking.

Screen Saver

Another option for watching and learning from other speakers is closer to home. Thanks to the Internet, spectacular speeches are just a click away. The beauty of watching or listening online is that you can hear it more than once. So, in this case, we suggest you watch the first time as a typical audience member. After the speech, notice how you are feeling about the speaker and his or her message. Then watch the speech again. This time, however, watch as a discerning active listener. You'll be able to find some great speeches on your own, but to help get you started we've assembled several of our favorites. We've purposely put together an eclectic mix to expose you to several different styles. You'll find speakers from the world of entertainment, sports, and politics. A few are even considered some of the best of the last 100 years! Though the content might not be your thing, the purpose of this particular activity is to evaluate delivery and speaking style. Refer to the previous list in the Watch and Learn section.

Speaker	Speech
Viola Davis	Acceptance Speech, 2015 Primetime Emmy Awards
Dame Stephanie Shirley	TED Talk: "Why Do Ambitious Women Have Flat Heads?" August 3, 2015
Senator Elizabeth Warren	Addressing U.S. Senate on Defunding Planned Parenthood, 2015
Dr. Rita Pierson	TED Talk: "Every Kid Needs a Champion," 2013
Representative Maureen Walsh	Address to Washington State Lawmakers on Gay Marriage, 2012
Former Secretary of State Condoleezza Rice	Keynote Address, 2012 Republican National Convention
Ellen DeGeneres	Commencement Address, 2009, Tulane University
Martin Sheen	Acceptance Speech, Notre Dame's Laetare Medal, 2008
Dr. Randy Pausch	"Really Achieving Your Childhood Dreams," 2007
Dixie Carter	Acceptance Speech, Evangeline Booth Award; The Salvation Army, 2007

Dr. Maya Angelou	Remarks at the Memorial Service for Coretta Scott King, 2006
Steve Jobs	Commencement Address, 2005, Stanford University
Jamie Foxx	Acceptance Speech, 2005, Academy Awards
Senator Daniel Inouye	Opening the National Museum of the American Indian, 2004
President Barack Obama	Keynote Address, 2004 Democratic National Convention
Senator Robert C. Byrd	"Arrogance of Power," 2003
Halle Berry	Acceptance Speech, 2002 Academy Awards
President Bill Clinton	Farewell Address to the Nation, 2001
Jim Valvano	Acceptance Speech, 1993 ESPY Award
Governor Ann Richards	Keynote Address, 1988 Democratic National Convention
President Ronald Reagan	Oval Office Address on the *Challenger* Disaster, 1986
Rev. Jesse Jackson	Keynote Address, 1984 Democratic National Convention

Congresswoman Barbara Jordan	Statement on the Articles of Impeachment, 1974
Dr. Martin Luther King, Jr.	"I Have a Dream," 1963
President John F. Kennedy	"Ask Not," Inaugural Address, 1961
Sir Winston Churchill	"We Shall Fight on the Beaches," 1940
Lou Gehrig	"Luckiest Man," 1939

Group Talk

Along with watching great speakers, the best way to get better is by doing. Fortunately, there are organizations that allow you to do just that. The following is a list of places that will help you develop your skills in a supportive environment. Check them out and find the one that suits you best.

- **Toastmasters International:** A nonprofit organization that helps develop public speaking and leadership skills through practice and feedback. You can find one in almost every city. Go to ToastMasters.org for more information.

- **Adult Extension Courses:** You can find courses specifically tailored for adult learners in all areas at most colleges and universities. Look for courses on Speech Communication, Speech, Public Speaking, or Oral Communication to help fine tune your skills.

- **Meetup:** An online social networking portal started in 2002 that facilitates in-person group meetings on various topics at locations around the world. People can sign up and attend a meeting already organized or develop one of their own and announce it on the Meetup Website. You may find a public speaking Meetup in your area or decide to start one of your own. Go to Meetup.com for more information.

Appendix

Anatomy of a Speech

We're often asked who our favorite speakers are and what we thought of this speech or that one. It's both hard and easy to answer. It's difficult because speaker styles and contexts vary so dramatically. And does "great" speaking equal admiration or effectiveness? For example, the question we get a lot is whether Adolf Hitler was a good speaker. Well, arguably, yes. He galvanized a nation with his words and dynamic delivery. He was also adept at appealing to the angst and frustration Germans felt after being defeated in World War I. On the other hand, Hitler's intentions were despicable and he used his oratory skills for nefarious purposes. See how evaluating can get tricky?

That being said, we do have perennial favorites like Ann Richards's speech at the 1988 Democratic Convention. More recently, Senator Elizabeth Warren (D–MA) delivered a new classic on the floor of the

U.S. Senate. What made these speeches so impressive to us? In this section, we'll tell you why we think they worked. Incidentally, both women were debaters in school.

Anatomy of a Speech: Gov. Ann Richards
Atlanta, GA
July 19, 1988

Ann Richards burst onto the national political stage when she delivered an electrifying keynote address at the 1988 Democratic National Convention. At the time, she was relatively unknown outside her native Texas, where she served as that state's treasurer. But on a July evening in Atlanta, the 54-year-old, white-haired Texan with the mega-watt wit stepped up to the podium and captivated a nation. She would go on to serve as the 45th governor of Texas. The speech she delivered that night at the DNC is often listed as one of the greatest speeches in modern times. We think it is one of the best, too. In a nutshell, it is a carefully crafted presentation delivered with zest, down home Southern charm, and memorable zingers.

Richards was known to only a handful of the more than 4,000 delegates from all over the United States when she stepped onto the stage. She, like the delegates, was a Democrat, but that seemed to be the only thing Richards had in common with them. How was she going to make a connection with so many different types of people from all over? What makes her introduction so truly remarkable is that she is able to personally connect with more than half the audience within the span of only 60 seconds. Let's look a little closer.

Thank you. Thank you. Thank you, very much.

Good evening, ladies and gentlemen. Buenas noches, mis amigos.

She spoke Spanish in the second sentence. If you're a Spanish speaker and suddenly you hear Spanish, your ears are going to perk up. You might think, "Hey, this woman is speaking my language. Let's see what she's all about."

I'm delighted to be here with you this evening, because after listening to George Bush all these years, I figured you needed to know what a real Texas accent sounds like.

By highlighting her Texas accent, she was speaking to Southerners in the room—and there were a lot of them. It was also a jab at George H.W. Bush, who was born in Massachusetts and raised in Connecticut.

Twelve years ago, Barbara Jordan, another Texas woman, made the keynote address to this convention, and two women in 160 years is about par for the course.

Barbara Jordan, also a formidable speaker in her own right, was an African-American woman. Richards deftly brought these groups of delegates—African Americans and women—into the conversation.

But if you give us a chance, we can perform. After all, Ginger Rogers did everything that Fred Astaire did. She just did it backwards and in high heels.

Richards puts a "button" on the point that women are more than capable and have been proving it for years. The point is, a woman's accomplishments sometimes go unnoticed.

I want to announce to this Nation that in a little more than 100 days, the Reagan-Meese-Deaver-Nofziger-Poindexter-North-Weinberger-Watt-Gorsuch-Lavelle-Stockman-Haig-Bork-Noriega-George Bush [era] will be over!

These are major political personalities from the era and represented what Democrats regarded as the Bush administration's failings. Richards received wild applause.

You know, tonight I feel a little like I did when I played basketball in the 8th grade. I thought I looked real cute in my uniform. And then I heard a boy yell from the bleachers, "Make that basket, bird legs." And my greatest fear is that same guy is somewhere out there in the audience tonight, and he's going to cut me down to size, because where I grew up there really wasn't much tolerance for self-importance, people who put on airs.

Richards showed vulnerability by telling this story, which made her human and relatable. This story transitioned beautifully into talking about small town Texas life and the values she grew up with.

I was born during the Depression in a little community just outside Waco, and I grew up listening to Franklin Roosevelt on the radio. Well, it was back then that I came to understand the small truths and the hardships that bind neighbors together. Those were real people with real problems and they had real dreams about getting out of the Depression. I can remember summer nights when we'd put down what we called the Baptist pallet and we listened to the grown-ups talk. I can still hear the sound of the dominoes clicking on the marble slab my daddy had found for a tabletop.

As we know, stories are powerful, and Richards told this story brilliantly, putting us in that backyard and yearning for a simpler time. The sound of the dominos adds an auditory element that made it multi-sensory. She also brings up FDR, an icon in American politics, a Democrat who led the country out of the Great Depression.

I can still hear the laughter of the men telling jokes you weren't supposed to hear—talkin' about how big that old buck deer was, laughin' about mama puttin' Clorox in the well when the frog fell in.

They talked about war and Washington and what this country needed. They talked straight talk. And it came from people who were living their lives as best they could. And that's what we're gonna do tonight. We're gonna tell how the cow ate the cabbage.

The colloquialism "how the cow ate the cabbage" was an excellent transition into her main arguments. Now, even if *you* don't know what that means, the audience she was speaking to did, which continued to increase her relatability and connection with them.

I got a letter last week from a young mother in Lorena, Texas, and I wanna read part of it to you. She writes,

"Our worries go from pay day to pay day, just like millions of others. And we have two fairly decent incomes, but I worry how I'm going to pay the rising car insurance and food. I pray my kids don't have a growth spurt from August to December, so I don't have to buy new jeans. We buy clothes at the budget stores and we have them fray and fade and stretch in the first wash. We ponder and try to figure out how we're gonna pay for college and braces and tennis shoes. We don't take vacations and we don't go out to eat. Please don't think me ungrateful. We have jobs and a nice place to live, and we're healthy. We're the people you see every day in the grocery stores, and we obey the laws. We pay our taxes. We fly our flags on holidays and we plod along trying to make it better for ourselves and our children and our parents. We aren't vocal anymore. I think maybe we're too tired. I believe that people like us are forgotten in America."

Richards read off what appeared to be the actual letter, thus lending authenticity. However, it was clear that she had the passage memorized and only referred to it occasionally. Illuminating a family's struggle did more than any statistic could and humanized the conditions of the working poor.

Well of course you believe you're forgotten, because you have been.

She talked back to the letter, but addressed the audience. This was a fantastic rhetorical strategy because it brought the discussion back into the arena.

> *This Republican Administration treats us as if we were pieces of a puzzle that can't fit together.*

Richards uses the analogy of a puzzle, which gives the audience a shortcut to her point.

> *They've tried to put us into compartments and separate us from each other. Their political theory is "divide and conquer." They've suggested time and time again that what is of interest to one group of Americans is not of interest to anyone else. We've been isolated. We've been lumped into that sad phraseology called "special interests."*

She sets up her argument that we are used as special interests before launching into several examples of how this is ultimately used against us.

> *They've told farmers that they were selfish, that they would drive up food prices if they asked the government to intervene on behalf of the family farm, and we watched farms go on the auction block while we bought food from foreign countries.*

> *Well, that's wrong!*

> *They told working mothers it's all their fault—their families are falling apart because they had to go to work to keep their kids in jeans and tennis shoes and college. And they're wrong!*

In the next section, Richards repeats the word *wrong* after each of her examples and she builds the momentum and energy of the word as she goes.

> *They told American labor they were trying to ruin free enterprise by asking for 60 days' notice of plant closings, and that's*

wrong. And they told the auto industry and the steel industry and the timber industry and the oil industry, companies being threatened by foreign products flooding this country, that you're "protectionist" if you think the government should enforce our trade laws. And that is wrong. When they belittle us for demanding clean air and clean water for trying to save the oceans and the ozone layer, that's wrong.

No wonder we feel isolated and confused. We want answers and their answer is that "something is wrong with you."

Well nothing's wrong with you.

Nothing's wrong with you that you can't fix in November!

Richards expertly takes a negative and makes it a positive.

We've been told—we've been told that the interests of the South and the Southwest are not the same interests as the North and the Northeast. They pit one group against the other. They've divided this country and, in our isolation, we think government isn't gonna help us, and we're alone in our feelings. We feel forgotten. Well, the fact is that we are not an isolated piece of their puzzle. We are one nation. We are the United States of America.

Now we Democrats believe that America is still the county of fair play, that we can come out of a small town or a poor neighborhood and have the same chance as anyone else; and it doesn't matter whether we are black or Hispanic or disabled or a women [sic]. We believe that America is a country where small business owners must succeed, because they are the bedrock, backbone of our economy.

One of the strongest ideals in America is one of fair play and equality. Richards uses this idea to her advantage. It hints to the story she told earlier in the speech about growing up in simpler times.

We believe that our kids deserve good daycare and public schools. We believe our kids deserve public schools where students can learn and teachers can teach. And we wanna believe that our parents will have a good retirement and that we will too. We Democrats believe that social security is a pact that cannot be broken.

We wanna believe that we can live out our lives without the terrible fear that an illness is going to bankrupt us and our children. We Democrats believe that America can overcome any problem, including the dreaded disease called AIDS. We believe that America is still a country where there is more to life than just a constant struggle for money. And we believe that America must have leaders who show us that our struggles amount to something and contribute to something larger—leaders who want us to be all that we can be.

Richards addresses a few of the major concerns Americans were facing at the time and, to some degree, still are.

We want leaders like Jesse Jackson. Jesse Jackson is a leader and a teacher who can open our hearts and open our minds and stir our very souls. And he has taught us that we are as good as our capacity for caring, caring about the drug problem, caring about crime, caring about education, and caring about each other.

Rev. Jesse Jackson is a noted African-American civil rights leader and by addressing him and his work, she tackles the race issue with ease.

Now, in contrast, the greatest nation of the free world has had a leader for eight straight years that has pretended that he cannot hear our questions over the noise of the helicopters. And we know he doesn't wanna answer. But we have a lot of questions. And when we get our questions asked, or there is a leak, or an investigation, the only answer we get is, "I don't know," or "I forgot."

This section refers to an ongoing feeling by many Democrats that the Bush administration avoided direct questions. The joke at the time was how reporters would ask the president questions as he boarded his helicopter, and he'd put his hand to his ear and signal as if he couldn't hear the question.

> *But you wouldn't accept that answer from your children. I wouldn't. "Don't tell me you 'don't know' or you 'forgot.'" We're not going to have the America that we want until we elect leaders who are gonna tell the truth; not most days, but every day; leaders who don't forget what they don't want to remember. And for eight straight years George Bush hasn't displayed the slightest interest in anything we care about. And now that he's after a job that he can't get appointed to, he's like Columbus discovering America. He's found child care. He's found education. Poor George. He can't help it. He was born with a silver foot in his mouth.*

This last line became one of her most famous zingers from this speech and, in fact, she was remembered for it throughout her career. It accomplished two things. It said that Bush was prone to misspeaking or not speaking at all, and that he grew up rich and couldn't relate to working people.

> *Well, no wonder. No wonder we can't figure it out. Because the leadership of this nation is telling us one thing on TV and doing something entirely different. They tell us—they tell us that they're fighting a war against terrorists. And then we find out that the White House is selling arms to the Ayatollah. They—they tell us that they're fighting a war on drugs and then people come on TV and testify that the CIA and the DEA and the FBI knew they were flying drugs into America all along. And they're negotiating with a dictator who is shoveling cocaine into this country like crazy. I guess that's their Central American strategy.*
>
> *Now they tell us that employment rates are great, and that they're for equal opportunity. But we know it takes two paychecks*

to make ends meet today, when it used to take one. And the opportunity they're so proud of is low-wage, dead-end jobs. And there is no major city in America where you cannot see homeless men sitting in parking lots holding signs that say, "I will work for food."

Now my friends, we really are at a crucial point in American history. Under this Administration we have devoted our resources into making this country a military colossus. But we've let our economic lines of defense fall into disrepair. The debt of this nation is greater than it has ever been in our history. We fought a world war on less debt than the Republicans have built up in the last eight years. You know, it's kind of like that brother-in-law who drives a flashy new car, but he's always borrowing money from you to make the payments.

Well, but let's take what they are most proudest of—that is their stand of defense. We Democrats are committed to a strong America and, quite frankly, when our leaders say to us, "We need a new weapons system," our inclination is to say, "Well, they must be right." But when we pay billions for planes that won't fly, billions for tanks that won't fire, and billions for systems that won't work, "that old dog won't hunt." And you don't have to be from Waco to know that when the Pentagon makes crooks rich and doesn't make America strong, that it's a bum deal.

Richards addresses a series of what Democrats perceived as Republican missteps and calls up her hometown of Waco, which at this point in the speech represents every small town in America.

Now I'm going to tell you, I'm really glad that our young people missed the Depression and missed the great Big War. But I do regret that they missed the leaders that I knew, leaders who told us when things were tough, and that we'd have to sacrifice, and that these difficulties might last for a while. They didn't tell us things were hard for us because we were different, or isolated, or special interests. They brought us together and they gave us a sense of national purpose. They gave us Social Security and they told us they were setting up a system where we could pay our own money in, and when the time came for our retirement we could take the money out. People in the rural areas were told that we deserved to have electric lights, and they were gonna harness the energy that was necessary to give us electricity so my grandmamma didn't have to carry that old coal oil lamp around. And they told us that they were gonna guarant[ee] when we put our money in the bank, that the money was going to be there, and it was going to be insured. They did not lie to us.

And I think one of the saving graces of Democrats is that we are candid. We talk straight talk. We tell people what we think. And that tradition and those values live today in Michael Dukakis from Massachusetts.

Richards gets to the solution for our country's woes: the Democratic candidate, Michael Dukakis.

Michael Dukakis knows that this country is on the edge of a great new era, that we're not afraid of change, that we're for thoughtful, truthful, strong leadership. Behind his calm there's an impatience to unify this country and to get on with the future. His instincts are deeply American. They're tough and they're generous. And personally, I have to tell you that I have never met a man who had a more remarkable sense about what is really important in life.

And then there's my friend and my teacher for many years, Senator Lloyd Bentsen. And I couldn't be prouder, both as a Texan and as a Democrat, because Lloyd Bentsen understands America. From the barrio to the boardroom, he knows how to bring us together, by regions, by economics, and by example. And he's already beaten George Bush once.

A great use of alliteration is shown in "From the barrio to the boardroom."

> *So, when it comes right down to it, this election is a contest between those who are satisfied with what they have and those who know we can do better. That's what this election is really all about. It's about the American dream—those who want to keep it for the few and those who know it must be nurtured and passed along.*

Richards clearly delineates the two major candidates.

> *I'm a grandmother now. And I have one nearly perfect granddaughter named Lily. And when I hold that grandbaby, I feel the continuity of life that unites us, that binds generation to generation, that ties us with each other. And sometimes I spread that Baptist pallet out on the floor, and Lily and I roll a ball back and forth. And I think of all the families like mine, like the one in Lorena, Texas, like the ones that nurture children all across America. And as I look at Lily, I know that it is within families that we learn both the need to respect individual human dignity and to work together for our common good. Within our families, within our nation, it is the same.*

She uses the phrase "Baptist pallet" which she used in one of her first stories, growing up outside Waco. Though it would be easy to miss, it triggers the same emotional response we felt moments earlier.

Instead of saying she spends time with her granddaughter Lily or just talks to her, Richards creates a compelling visual of rolling a ball back and forth between them. It's also a useful metaphor about passing the ball to the next generation.

Finally, she talks about the young letter writer from Lorena, Texas, who puts a human face on the day-to-day struggles of so many people.

> *And as I sit there, I wonder if she'll ever grasp the changes I've seen in my life—if she'll ever believe that there was a time when blacks could not drink from public water fountains, when*

Hispanic children were punished for speaking Spanish in the public schools, and women couldn't vote.

Here, Richards circles back to her memorable attention-getter: the Spanish speakers, African Americans, and the capabilities of women.

I think of all the political fights I've fought, and all the compromises I've had to accept as part payment. And I think of all the small victories that have added up to national triumphs and all the things that would never have happened and all the people who would've been left behind if we had not reasoned and fought and won those battles together. And I will tell Lily that those triumphs were Democratic Party triumphs.

She reinforces that the Democrats fight even against the greatest of odds and the bitterness of defeats.

I want so much to tell Lily how far we've come, you and I. And as the ball rolls back and forth, I want to tell her how very lucky she is that for all our difference, we are still the greatest nation on this good earth. And our strength lies in the men and women who go to work every day, who struggle to balance their family and their jobs, and who should never, ever be forgotten.

She doesn't drop the ball. She brings it up again. Whereas lesser speakers might have let it go, she continues to use it as a metaphor.

I just hope that like her grandparents and her great-grandparents before that, Lily goes on to raise her kids with the promise that echoes in homes all across America: that we can do better, and that's what this election is all about.

Richards's conclusion is extremely personal, but highly relatable. Her last line encapsulates her entire speech.

Thank you very much.

Anatomy of a Speech: U.S. Senator Elizabeth Warren (D–MA)

Washington D.C.

August 3, 2015

Planned Parenthood was in the news a lot in 2015. A lot. Widely circulated and heavily edited "undercover videos" seemed to show that the nonprofit organization was engaged in the illegal activity of selling baby body parts. Despite the fact that this is not, and has never been, the case, the videos became an instant political lightening rod. For years, Planned Parenthood has been a target of the pro-life movement for offering abortion services. As false impressions swirled feverishly, Republican Congress members were pressured by conservative groups to take legislative action. On the eve of a vote to defund Planned Parenthood, Elizabeth Warren, a rising star of the Democratic Party and senator from Massachusetts, addressed her colleagues from the floor of the U.S. Senate. Her clear and compelling argument coupled with a dynamic and confident delivery made her speech an instant classic. The vote to defund Planned Parenthood was defeated.

I come to the Senate floor today to ask my Republican colleagues a question: Do you have any idea what year it is? Did you fall down, hit your head, and think you woke up in the 1950s? Or the 1890s?

Should we call for a doctor? Because I simply cannot believe that in the year 2015, the United States Senate would be spending its time trying to defund women's healthcare centers.

Warren opens with a pointed question, mockingly implying that the only way Republicans can be pushing this vote is if they had totally lost their minds.

You know, on second thought, maybe I shouldn't be surprised. The Republicans have had a plan for years to strip away women's rights to make choices over our own bodies. Just look at the recent facts.

Warren then takes the opportunity to address a history of legislation meant to take away a woman's right to choose.

In 2013, Republicans threatened to shut down the government unless they could change the law to let employers deny women access to birth control.

In March of this year, Republicans held up a non-controversial bipartisan bill to stop human trafficking. Why? Because they demanded new anti-abortion restrictions to cover private funding meant to help the victims of human trafficking.

In the previous passage, Warren shows the "all or nothing" approach to anti-abortion restrictions Republicans are willing to go to even in the most dire of circumstances—in this case, human trafficking.

In June, House Republicans passed a budget eliminating funding for the Title X family planning program—the only federal grant program that provides birth control, HIV tests, STD screening, and other preventive services for poor and uninsured people.

Now, Warren demonstrates how much is really at stake if Planned Parenthood is defunded. The poor and uninsured people are hurt the most.

Over the past few years, Republicans have voted to repeal the Affordable Care Act more than 50 times, including the portions that require insurers to cover contraception.

And let's be clear: it's not just Congress. Over the past five years, Republican state legislators have passed nearly 300 new restrictions on abortion access. This year alone, Republican state legislators have passed more than 50 new restrictions on women's access to legal healthcare.

Warren trots out the numbers. And they are meant to shock.

So Madam President, let's be really clear about something. The Republican scheme to defund Planned Parenthood is not some sort of surprised response to a highly edited video. Nope! The Republican vote to defund Planned Parenthood is just one more piece of a deliberate, methodical, orchestrated, rightwing attack on women's rights. And I'm sick and tired of it. Women everywhere are sick and tired of it. The American people are sick and tired of it.

The Senator's thesis is that this isn't about videos; it's about a systemic and concerted effort to take away a woman's right to choose. She also reminds Republican Senators that there are people not aligned with the pro-life lobby who vote, especially women.

Scheduling this vote during the week of a big Fox News presidential primary debate, days before candidates take trips to Iowa or New Hampshire isn't just some clever gimmick.

This is an all-out effort to build support to take away a woman's right to control her own body and access to medical care she may need.

Warren eliminates the notion that this is simply political grand standing but rather, again, an orchestrated effort on the part of Republicans to dismantle abortion rights in the United States.

Now this affects all of us. Whatever your age, wherever you live, I guarantee that you know someone who has used Planned Parenthood health centers. No one may mention it at Thanksgiving dinner or paste it on Facebook for the whole world to know. But just look at the facts. One in five women in America is a Planned Parenthood patient at least once in her life. Every single year, nearly 2.7 million women and men show up for help at Planned Parenthood.

Warren connects the Senators and the television audience with this issue. She makes it personal by noting that we have gone to Planned Parenthood ourselves, or know someone who has. It might not be discussed in polite conversation, but that doesn't mean it isn't happening. This invisible and silent population benefits greatly and, yes, they vote, too.

Why do so many people use Planned Parenthood? Because they're nonprofit and they're open. More than half of Planned Parenthood centers are located in areas without ready access to healthcare.

Warren brings up Planned Parenthood's nonprofit status and the access to medical care it provides to rural areas of the country.

Women who can't get appointments anywhere else go to Planned Parenthood for pap tests and cancer screening. Couples go to Planned Parenthood for STD treatments or pregnancy tests. Young people go to Planned Parenthood for birth control.

And yes, 3 percent of patients visit Planned Parenthood for a safe and legal abortion, with a doctor who will show compassion and care for a woman who is making one of the most difficult decisions of her entire life.

The Senator uses this opportunity to talk about the many services beyond abortion, but doesn't skirt that issue either. She makes a point to use the words "safe" and "legal" when she says that only 3 percent of patients visit Planned Parenthood for abortions. She also makes this number emotional by saying it is the "most difficult" decision of a woman's life.

But just to be clear, even though the abortions performed at Planned Parenthood are safe and legal, the federal government is not paying for any of them. Not. One. Dime.

For almost 40 years, the federal government has prohibited federal funding for abortions, except in the case of rape, incest, or life endangerment. Most of the money Planned Parenthood receives from the government comes in the form of Medicaid patients, for medical care provided to low-income patients. The same payments that any other doctor or clinic receives for providing cancer screenings or other medical exams.

The rest of Planned Parenthood's federal funding comes from Title X. It provides birth control to low-income and uninsured people. The same program the House Republicans voted to cut in June.

The government doesn't fund abortions. Period.

Now, Warren delivers the knockout punch. Again, she uses the words "safe" and "legal." Then she makes it clear that the federal government doesn't fund abortions at Planned Parenthood and never has.

A vote today to defund Planned Parenthood is not a vote to defund abortions. It's a vote to defund cancer screenings and birth control and basic healthcare for millions of women.

Warren then shows the real consequences of defunding Planned Parenthood: Women across America will lose basic healthcare.

I want to say to my Republican colleagues: the year is 2015. Not 1955 and not 1895.

She returns to her attention-getter in her conclusion.

Women have lived through a world where backward-looking ideologues tried to interfere with the basic health decisions made by a woman and her doctor, and we are not going back. Not now, not ever.

Warren's battle cry: We're not going backward.

The Republican plan to defund Planned Parenthood is a Republican plan to defund women's healthcare. For my daughter, for my granddaughters, for people all across Massachusetts and all across this country, I stand with Planned Parenthood. And I hope my colleagues will do the same.

Generations of women are affected, not only in the state Warren represents, but also throughout the nation. Saying she "stands" with Planned Parenthood is a powerful image. It's solidarity, yes, but it's also a U.S. senator saying that if you want to take away a woman's right to choose, you're going to have to take me down, too—and I'm not going anywhere.

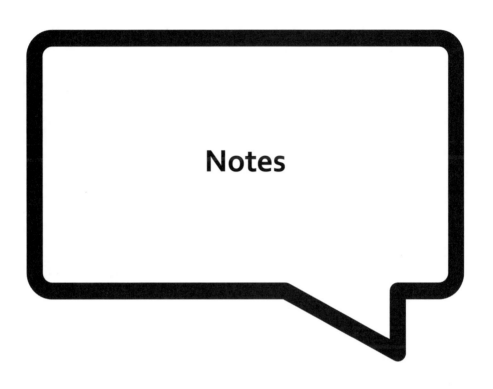

Notes

Chapter 1

1. Michael Bay is a prolific feature film director and producer. He is best known for big-budget action movies including: *Transformers*, *Pearl Harbor*, and *Armageddon*. BoxOfficeMojo.com. IMDB.com, 2015. Web. Oct. 2015.

2. Bay was on hand to help introduce a new curved screen by Samsung. The news of his fumbled presentation hit social media immediately, with the video going viral. Andrea Chang and Salvador Rodriguez, "CES 2014 live: Michael Bay 'embarrassed' by meltdown on stage," LATimes.com. Tribune Publishing Company, 2014. Web. 6 Jan. 2014.

3. Career advice columnist Jay Leader writes, "Public speaking is a critical skill that is valuable to anyone, regardless of their general duties or responsibilities." Jay Leader, "Why public speaking is a critical skill," Computerworld.com. IDG Communications, 2011. Web. 8 April 2011.

4. Jay Ingraham, "America's top fears: Public speaking, heights and bugs," WashingtonPost.com. Nash Hollings, LLC, 2014. Web. 30 Oct. 2014.

5. Rob Dunn, "What Are You So Scared of? Saber-Toothed Cats, Snakes, and Carnivorous Kangaroos," Slate.com. The Slate Group, 2012. Web. 15 Oct. 2012.

6. Early humans were nomadic hunter-gatherers. An agricultural revolution began roughly 12,000 years ago, transiting these once mobile populations to sedentary societies based on crop production. Graeme Barker, *The Agricultural Revolution in Prehistory: Why did Foragers become Farmers?* (Oxford: Oxford UP, 2009).

7. Jon Hamilton, "From Primitive Parts, A Highly Evolved Brain," NPR.com. National Public Radio, Inc., 2010. Web. 9 Aug. 2010.

8. Natalie Angier, "So Much More Than Plasma and Poison," NYTimes.com. The New York Times Company, 2011. Web. 6 June 2011.

9. Lydia DePillis, "Lots of Americans fear flying. But not because of plane crashes," WashingtonPost.com. Nash Hollings, LLC, 2014. Web. 31 Dec. 2014.

10. "Commercial aviation [is] the safest mode of travel in the United States." There are 0.07 fatalities per billion passenger miles. The majority of aviation fatalities that occur each year (85 percent) involve private aircraft. On average, 549 people die each year through recreational flying (41 percent), business travel (24 percent), and instruction (17 percent). Leighton Walter Kille, "Transportation safety over time: Cars, planes,

trains, walking, cycling," JournalistsResources.org. Harvard Kennedy School, Shorenstein Center on Media, Politics and Public Policy, 2014. Web. 5 Oct. 2014.

11. Chicago-based psychologist David Carbonell runs anxiety-management workshops for fearful fliers. He says, "There's a social phobia aspect. [My clients are] afraid they will look so intensely nervous that they will alienate everybody in the airplane. They're afraid they're going to look weird." Sophia Dembling, "Inner Turbulence: Don't let fear of flying get in the way of your business," Entrepreneur.com. Entrepreneur Media, Inc., 2013. Dec. 2013.

12. This quote is widely attributed to Mark Twain. Jerry Weissman, "Another Humorous View on the Fear of Public Speaking," Forbes.com. Forbes, Inc., 2014. Web. 17 June 2014.

13. Barbara Schmidt, "Chronology of Known Mark Twain Speeches, Public Readings, and Lectures," TwainQuotes.com. Web. 28 Oct. 2015.

14. The description for the book claims the author has "the proven method for overcoming your fear of public speaking and delivering dynamic presentations" and says he "explains how the brain processes information." The author holds a BS in International Relations and French and there is no evidence he has any scientific, psychology, medical, or academic communication credentials. Bill Hoogterp, *Your Perfect Presentation: Speak in Front of Any Audience Anytime Anywhere and Never Be Nervous Again* (New York: McGraw-Hill Education, 2014).

15. Homo sapiens began to evolve around 200,000 years ago. "History of life on earth," BBC.co.uk. British Broadcasting Corporation, 2014. Web. Oct. 2014.

16. "Common Signs & Signals of Stress Reaction," Foh.dhhs. gov. U.S. Department of Health and Human Services, 2015. Web. 30, Oct. 2015.

17. Amy Cuddy, "Your Body Language Shapes Who You Are," online video clip, TED.com. Sapling Foundation, 2012. June 2012.

Chapter 2

1. This study found that self-talk affects only the cognitive process, helps people to remember what they are searching for, and helps via word-to-word matching. Gary Lupyan and Daniel Swingley, "Self-directed speech affects visual search performance," *The Quarterly Journal of Experimental Psychology*, 65.6 (June 2012): 1068–1085.

2. The authors conclude that self-talk is effective in sports and encourage its use as a strategy to learn and enhance performance. Antonis Hatzigeorgiadis, et al, "Self-Talk and Sports Performance: A Meta-Analysis," *Perspectives on Psychological Science*, 6.4 (July 2011): 348–356.

3. Psychologists Robert Firestone and Lisa Firestone study what they call the "critical inner voice" and have published extensively on the topic. Robert W. Firestone, et al, *Conquer Your Critical Inner Voice: A Revolutionary Program to Counter Negative Thoughts and Live Free from Imagined Limitations* (Oakland, CA: New Harbinger Publications, May 2012).

4. Although scholars believe woolly mammoths disappeared from most of the world starting 10,000 years ago, a small population survived on Wrangel Island in the Arctic Ocean until 2,000 BC. Dhruti Shah, "Mammoth's extinction not due to inbreeding, study finds," BBC.co.uk. British Broadcasting Company, 2012. Web. 23 March 2012.

5. Rick Hanson, "Wake Up to Good News," *The Huffington Post*. TheHuffingtonPost.com, 13 Aug. 2013. Web. 2 Oct. 2015.

6. A study at the Harvard Medical Lab found that "mental practice" can alter the physical structure and function of the brain. Sharon Begley, "The Brain: How the Brain Rewires Itself," Time.com. Time Inc., 2007. Web. 19 Jan. 2007.

7. Elisha Goldstein, "If You Can Name It, You Can Tame It," *Mindfulness and Psychotherapy*. Psych Central, 6 Jan. 2014. Web. 19 Oct. 2015.

8. A.J. LeVan, "Seeing Is Believing: The Power of Visualization," *Psychology Today*, 3 Dec. 2009. Web. 8 Aug. 2015.

Chapter 3

1. "Letter from Wallace, A.R. to Darwin, C.R. (July 2, 1866)," DarwinProject.ac.uk, University of Cambridge. Web. 30 Oct. 2015.

2. "Life Expectancy," CDC.gov. Centers for Disease Control and Prevention, 2015. Web. 30, Oct. 2015.

3. FDR gave this advice on public speaking to his son James Roosevelt. Paul L. Soper, *Basic Public Speaking* (Oxford: Oxford UP, 1963).

4. Abraham Lincoln is said to have used a similar phrase in a speech in Clinton, Illinois on September 2, 1858, but historians have disputed this. The version of this phrase is also attributed to John Lydgate of Bury (1370–1451), a monk and poet. Still others claim showman P.T. Barnum is the source.

Chapter 4

1. The Brothers Grimm "sought the purist form of straightforward narration.... They realized the educational value of stories." William Harrer, "The Value of Grimm's Fairy

Tales," WaldorfLibrary.org. Research Institute for Waldorf Education. Web. 14 Nov. 2014.

2. Joseph Campbell, *The Hero with a Thousand Faces* (Novato, CA: New World Library, July 2008).

3. "American Masters: George Lucas," online video, PBS.org. Public Broadcasting Service, March 1993.

4. Ishaan Tharoor, "Before Noah: Myths of the Flood Are Far Older Than the Bible," Time.com. Time Inc., 2014. Web. 1 April 2014.

5. "Story of Noah," Genesis 6:9, *Good News Bible: The Bible in Today's English Version* (New York: American Bible Society, 1976).

6. Leo Widrich, "The Science of Storytelling: Why Telling a Story is the Most Powerful Way to Activate our Brains," LifeHacker.com. Gawker Media, 2012. Web. 12 Dec. 2012.

7. Jonathan Gottschall, "Why Storytelling Is The Ultimate Weapon," Co.Create. Fast Company, Inc., 2 May 2012. Web. 2 July 2015.

8. Jeremy Hsu, "The Secrets of Storytelling: Why We Love a Good Yarn," ScientificAmerican.com. Nature Publishing Group, 2008. Web. 8 Sept. 2008.

9. Nicole Sperling, "With help from a friend, Mel cut to the chase," WashingtonPost.com. Nash Hollings, LLC, 2006. Web. 15 Dec. 2006.

10. "David and Goliath," 1 Samuel 17: 1–58, *Good News Bible: The Bible in Today's English Version* (New York: American Bible Society, 1976).

11. The article notes: "Duke is a Champion today, but Butler is a winner." Lenn Robbins, "Butler's underdogs triumphant in defeat," NYPost.com. News Corp, 2010. Web. 7 April 2010.

12. This interview features Dr. Nadav Goldschmied who studies Social Psychology at the University of San Diego, Dr.

Scott T. Allison, Professor of Psychology at the University of Richmond, and Daniel Engber who laments his penchant for supporting the underdog. "Games," *RadioLab*, NPR. 23 Aug. 2011. Radio.

13. Ryan Niemiec, "The Psychology of the Underdog," *Character Strengths*, PsychCentral.com, 19 Mar. 2012. Web. 29 Oct. 2015.

14. Katy Waldman, "Sunshine, Baseball, and Etch A Sketch: How Politicians Use Analogies," Slate.com. The Slate Group, 23 Sept. 2014. Web. 1 Oct. 2015.

15. "Franklin D. Roosevelt," *HISTORY*, AETN. Web. 1 Nov. 2015.

16. "Questions over Greg Mortenson's Stories," CBSNews.com. CBS Interactive, 19 Apr. 2011. Web. 2 Oct. 2015.

17. Matt Pearce, "'Three Cups' Author Greg Mortenson Must Pay $1 Million to Charity," *Los Angeles Times*, 5 Apr. 2012.

Chapter 5

1. Ronald B. Adler and Lawrence B. Rosenfeld, "Interpersonal Communication and Self," *Interplay: The Process of Interpersonal Communication*. Thirteenth ed. (Oxford UP, 2015). 72, 73.

2. Ibid., 71.

3. "Identity Management Theory," *Communication Theory RSS*. Web. 1 Nov. 2015.

4. Chip Heath and Dan Heath, *Made to Stick: Why Some Ideas Survive and Others Die* (New York: Random House, 2007).

5. Marco Iacoboni, *Mirroring People: The New Science of How We Connect with Others* (New York: Farrar, Straus and Giroux, 2008).

Chapter 6

1. "Francis Bacon," Bio.com, A&E Networks Television. Web. 1 Nov. 2015.

2. Mihaly Csikszentmihalyi, *Flow: The Psychology of Optimal Experience* (New York: Harper Perennial Modern Classics, 2008).

3. "Top 10 Tips for QSR Suggestive Selling," QSRweb.com. 18 Mar. 2010. Web. 1 Nov. 2015.

4. Jeff Thompson, "Is Nonverbal Communication a Numbers Game?" *Psychology Today*, 30 Sept. 2011. Web. 1 Nov. 2015.

Chapter 7

1. David Rock and Jeffrey Schwartz, "The Neuroscience of Leadership," *Strategy Business*. PWC, 30 May 2006. Web. 7 Oct. 2015.

2. Evian Gordon, *Integrative Neuroscience: Bringing Together Biological, Psychological and Clinical Models of the Human Brain* (Amsterdam: Harwood Academic, 2000).

3. Robert Siegel, Melissa Block, and Mark Liberman, "In 'Um' Or 'Uh,' A Few Clues To What We're Saying—And Who's Saying It," NPR, 12 Aug. 2014. Web. 1 Sept. 2015.

4. There is some debate of the actual origins of Uptalk, but researchers have looked to Southern California, Australia, and New Zealand as the most likely candidates. "The Unstoppable March of the Upward Inflection?" BBC News, British Broadcasting Company, 11 Aug. 2014. Web. 1 Oct. 2015.

5. The UK publisher, Pearson, surveyed 700 managers. More than half said a high-rising terminal would hinder their prospects and 85 percent said the trait was a "clear indicator of insecurity." "Want a Promotion? Don't Speak like an

AUSSIE: Rising in Pitch at the End of Sentences Make You Sound 'insecure,'" *Mail Online*. Associated Newspapers, 13 Jan. 2014. Web. 1 Nov. 2015.

6. Sue Langley, "The Neuroscience of Change: Why It's Difficult and What Makes It Easier," *Langley Group*, 23 May 2012. Web. 9 Aug. 2015.

Chapter 8

1. Francis Flynn, "Francis Flynn: What Makes People Want to Help Others?" *Stanford Graduate School of Business*, 21 Nov. 2013. Web. 15 Aug. 2015.

2. N. Howlett, K.L. Pine, I. Orakçıoğlu, and B. Fletcher, "The Influence of Clothing on First Impressions: Rapid and Positive Responses to Minor Changes in Male Attire," *Journal of Fashion Marketing and Management* (2013): 38–48.

3. N. Howlett, K.L. Pine, I. Orakçıoğlu, and B. Fletcher, "Small Changes in Clothing Equal Big Changes in Perception: The Interaction between Provocativeness and Occupational Status," *Sex Roles: A Journal of Research* 72.3–4 (2015): 105–16.

4. Adam Haro and Adam Galinsky, "Enclothed Cognition," *Journal of Experimental Social Psychology* 48.4 (2012): 918–25.

5. Judith Sjo-Gaber, "The Real Cost of a Fabulous Smile: Put Your Best Smile Forward," Bloomberg.com. Web. 1 Nov. 2015.

Chapter 9

1. Stephen Shankland, "Moore's Law: The Rule That Really Matters in Tech," CNET.com. 15 Oct. 2012. Web. 1 Nov. 2015.

2. Charles Duhigg, *The Power of Habit: Why We Do What We Do in Life and Business* (New York: Random House, 2012).

3. "Flyers History: Kate Smith," FlyersHistory.com. Web. 1 Nov. 2015.

4. Leon Festinger, *A Theory of Cognitive Dissonance* (Stanford: Stanford U, 1985).

5. "To Savor the Flavor, Perform a Short Ritual First," *Association for Psychological Science RSS*. Web. 1 Nov. 2015.

6. Tracy Epton and Peter R. Harris, "Self-affirmation Promotes Health Behavior Change," *Health Psychology* 27.6 (2008): 746–52.

7. Hara Marano, "Our Brain's Negative Bias," *Psychology Today*, 29 Oct. 2010. Web. 2 Oct. 2015.

8. Max Gunther, Steven Beach, Nathan Yanasak, and L. Stephen Miller, "Deciphering Spousal Intentions: An FMRI Study of Couple Communication," *Journal of Social and Personal Relationships* 26.4 (2009): 388–410.

9. Rick Nauert, "Why We Want to Do the Opposite of Our Spouses' Wishes," *Psych Central News*. Psych Central. Web. 1 Nov. 2015.

10. Stephanie Pappas, "Even Grown-Ups Need Security Blankets," *LiveScience*, TechMedia Network, 10 Oct. 2010. Web. 1 Nov. 2015.

Chapter 10

1. Caitlin Johnson, "Cutting Through Advertising Clutter," CBSNews.com. CBS Interactive, 17 Sept. 2006. Web. 2 Nov. 2015.

2. "The Power of Categories," NPR.com, 6 Feb. 2015. Web. 18 Aug. 2015.

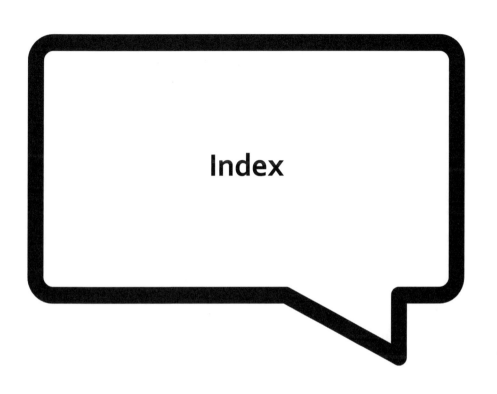

Index

About the Authors

Steve Rohr is an entertainment public relations executive and college professor. He is founder and president of Lexicon Public Relations and is the Show Publicist for the Oscars®. Steve's involvement in public speaking education spans two decades. For three years, he cohosted a psychology radio show with Dr. Shirley Impellizzeri. Steve earned his BA in communication and political science from Concordia College (Moorhead) and his MA in communication from Arizona State University. This is his first book.

Dr. Shirley Impellizzeri is one of America's most recognized Latina psychologists. She is a frequent guest expert on shows such as *Dr. Drew* and *The Doctors*, and cohosted a psychology radio show with Steve Rohr. She maintains a thriving private practice in Beverly Hills, California. She earned her PhD in psychology from UCLA. Shirley is the author of the bestselling *Why Can't I Change? How to Conquer Your Self-Destructive Patterns*.